LEAN & GREEN DIET COOKBOOK

THE NEW DIET PROGRAM TO BOOST YOUR WEIGHT LOSS WITH MORE THAN 100 AFFORDABLE AND EASY RECIPES. KICKSTART YOUR LONG-TERM TRANSFORMATION AND LOSE WEIGHT EFFICIENTLY.

ISABELLA HILL

CONTENTS

Legal Notice	ix
Disclaimer Notice	xi
Introduction	xiii

1. What Is the Optavia Diet? — 1
2. Exercise and The Optavia Diet? — 6
3. How Optavia Diet Can Help You — 9
4. Possible Downsides of the Optavia Diet — 12

LEAN AND GREEN RECIPES (BREAKFAST)

1. Tasty Breakfast Donuts — 21
2. Cheesy Spicy Bacon Bowls — 23
3. Goat Cheese Zucchini Kale Quiche — 25
4. Cream Cheese Egg Breakfast — 27
5. Avocado Red Peppers Roasted Scrambled Eggs — 28
6. Mushroom Quickie Scramble — 30
7. Coconut Coffee and Ghee — 32
8. Yummy Veggie Waffles — 34
9. Omega 3 Breakfast Shake — 36
10. Bacon Spaghetti Squash Carbonara — 38
11. Lime Bacon Thyme Muffins — 40
12. Gluten -Free Pancakes — 42
13. Mushroom & Spinach Omelet — 44

LEAN AND GREEN RECIPES (LUNCH)

14. Tomatillo and Green Chili Pork Stew — 49
15. Optavia Cloud Bread — 51

16. Avocado Lime Shrimp Salad	53
17. Broccoli Cheddar Breakfast Bake	55
18. Grilled Mahi Mahi with Jicama Slaw	57
19. Rosemary Cauliflower Rolls	59
20. Mediterranean Chicken Salad	61

LEAN AND GREEN RECIPES (DINNER) MEAT AND FISH

21. Chipotle Chicken & Cauliflower Rice Bowls	65
22. Lemon Garlic Oregano Chicken with Asparagus	67
23. Sheet Pan Chicken Fajita Lettuce Wraps	69
24. Savory Cilantro Salmon	71
25. Salmon Florentine	73
26. Tomato Braised Cauliflower with Chicken	75
27. Cheeseburger Soup	77
28. Braised Collard Greens in Peanut Sauce with Pork Tenderloin	79

LEAN AND GREEN RECIPES (DINNER) VEGETARIAN

29. Taste of Normandy Salad	83
30. Loaded Caesar Salad with Crunchy Chickpeas	85
31. Coleslaw worth a Second Helping	87
32. Romaine Lettuce and Radicchios Mix	89
33. Greek Salad	91
34. Asparagus and Smoked Salmon Salad	93
35. Shrimp Cobb Salad	95
36. Toast with Smoked Salmon, Herbed Cream Cheese, and Greens	97
37. Crab Melt with Avocado and Egg	99
38. Crispy Potatoes with Smoked Salmon, Kale, and Hollandaise-Style Sauce	101

LEAN AND GREEN RECIPES (DESSERT)

39. Faro with Artichoke Hearts — 105
40. Rice and Spinach — 107
41. Spiced Couscous — 109
42. Sweet Potato Mash — 111
43. Tabbouleh — 113
44. Orzo with Spinach and Feta — 115
45. Pasta Puttanesca — 117
46. Pasta with Pesto — 119
47. Sun-Dried Tomato and Artichoke Pizza — 121

LEAN AND GREEN RECIPES (SNACKS)

48. Veggie Fritters — 127
49. White Bean Dip — 129
50. Eggplant Dip — 131
51. Bulgur Lamb Meatballs — 133
52. Cucumber Bites — 135
53. Stuffed Avocado — 136
54. Hummus with Ground Lamb — 138
55. Wrapped Plums — 140
56. Cucumber Sandwich Bites — 141
57. Cucumber Rolls — 143
58. Olives and Cheese Stuffed Tomatoes — 144
59. Tomato Salsa — 146
60. Chili Mango and Watermelon Salsa — 148
61. Creamy Spinach and Shallots Dip — 150
62. Feta Artichoke Dip — 151
63. Avocado Dip — 153
64. Goat Cheese and Chives Spread — 154

FUELING RECIPES (BREAKFAST)

65. Lettuce Salad with Beef Strips	157
66. Cayenne Rib Eye Steak	159
67. Beef-Chicken Meatball Casserole	161
68. Juicy Pork Chops	163
69. Chicken Goulash	165
70. Chicken & Turkey Meatloaf	167
71. Turkey Meatballs with Dried Dill	169
72. Chicken Coconut Poppers	171
73. Parmesan Beef Slices	173
74. Chili Beef Jerky	175
75. Spinach Beef Heart	177

FUELING RECIPES (MAIN MEAL)

76. Parmesan Zucchini Rounds	181
77. Green Bean Casserole	183
78. Zucchini Spaghetti	185
79. Cabbage and Radishes Mix	186
80. Kale Chips	188
81. Coriander Artichokes	189
82. Spinach and Artichokes Sauté	190
83. Green Beans	191
84. Balsamic Cabbage	192
85. Herbed Radish Sauté	193
86. Roasted Tomatoes	194
87. Kale and Walnuts	196
88. Bok Choy and Butter Sauce	198
89. Turmeric Mushroom	199

FUELING RECIPES (SNACKS AND DESSERT)

90. Chocolate Bars	203
91. Blueberry Muffins	205
92. Chia Pudding	207
93. Avocado Pudding	209

94. Peanut Butter Coconut Popsicle	210
95. Delicious Brownie Bites	211
96. Pumpkin Balls	213
97. Smooth Peanut Butter Cream	215
98. Vanilla Avocado Popsicles	216
99. Chocolate Popsicle	218
100. Raspberry Ice Cream	220
101. Chocolate Frosty	221
102. Chocolate Almond Butter Brownie	223
103. Peanut Butter Fudge	225
104. Almond Butter Fudge	227
Conclusion	229

© Copyright 2021 by Isabella Hill- All rights reserved.

The content contained within this book may not be reproduced, duplicated or transmitted without direct written permission from the author or the publisher.

Under no circumstances will any blame or legal responsibility be held against the publisher, or author, for any damages, reparation, or monetary loss due to the information contained within this book. Either directly or indirectly.

LEGAL NOTICE

This book is copyright protected. This book is only for personal use. You cannot amend, distribute, sell, use, quote or paraphrase any part, or the content within this book, without the consent of the author or publisher.

DISCLAIMER NOTICE

Please note the information contained within this document is for educational and entertainment purposes only. All effort has been executed to present accurate, up to date, and reliable, complete information. No warranties of any kind are declared or implied. Readers acknowledge that the author is not engaging in the rendering of legal, financial, medical or professional advice. The content within this book has been derived from various sources. Please consult a licensed professional before attempting any techniques outlined in this book.

By reading this document, the reader agrees that under no circumstances is the author responsible for any losses, direct or indirect, which are incurred as a result of the use of information contained within this document, including, but not limited to, errors, omissions, or inaccuracies.

INTRODUCTION

The Optavia diet is designed to help people lose weight and fat by reducing calories and carbohydrates through portion-controlled meals and snacks.

Between 6 portioned-controlled meals, the 5&1 plan limits the calories to 800-1,000 calories per day.

There is no intact research about it. Many studies also show more significant weight loss with full or partial meal replacement plans than traditional calorie-restricted diets.

A lot of researches also revealed that reducing the total intake of calories is effective for weight loss. The low carb diets are also included here.

A study was conducted for 16 weeks, having 198 participants with excess weight or obesity. They found out that Optavia 5&1 Plan had significantly lower weight, waist circumference, and fat levels than the control group.

The research suggested additional benefits since it resulted in a right way. It associates 5-10 % weight loss with a reduced risk of heart disease and also types two diabetes. Those who also tried the 5&1 Plan lost 5.7% of their body weight, on average, having a percentage of 28.1 % of participants losing over 105.

Introduction

It is also said that one-on-one coaching is constructive, as well. A similar study was also conducted regarding it. They found out that individuals on the 5&1 diet who have completed at least 75% of the coaching sessions had lost more than twice their original weight, unlike those who only participated in fewer sessions.

All the same, many significant and related studies have also demonstrated and resulted in a substantial improvement with short and long-term weight loss. The diet adherence in programs that includes ongoing coaching is also included in it.

But then, currently, there are no studies yet that have proven the long term results of the famous Optavia diet. Still, research conducted similar to the Medifast plan noted that the percentage of participants who have maintained the diet for a year was 25%.

Another research also showed some of them regain weight during the weight maintenance phase while following another diet called the 5&1 Medifast diet. Coaching is the only factor that differs from the 5&1 Medifast diet and the 5&1 Optavia Plan. Overall, it is inevitable that more research is needed to assess the Optavia diet's lifetime effectiveness.

The low calorie and low carbohydrates plan of the Optavia diet is continuously gathering support from experts since it has been proven to show a temporary fat and weight loss. In the future, if more research and study will be done, its long-term effectiveness will now be defined.

The Optavia diet is considered a high-protein diet, having a protein that counts up to 10–35% of a person's daily calories. Nevertheless, powdered, processed substances can result in some unpleasant consequences.

According to London, "The additives and protein isolate plus can give you some unnecessary GI side effects that can make an individual feel bloated, making it a lot better with a sugar-free Greek yogurt that contains protein in a smoothie." Also, according to London, "there is no regulation of dietary supplements like powders and shakes for safety by the FDA as there is for foods. Protein blends and powders can contain unwanted ingredients and can interfere with your medication. This makes it important to inform your doctor about what you are trying to indulge yourself in".

1
WHAT IS THE OPTAVIA DIET?

The Optavia Diet is the brainchild of the man behind the multimillion-dollar company Medifast– Dr. William Vitale. Now carrying the brand Optavia since 2017, the goal of this diet is to encourage healthy and sustainable weight loss among its clientele. While there are many types of diet regimen that are available in the market, the Optavia Diet is ranked in the top 30 Best Diets in the United States.

Under this diet regimen, dieters are required to follow a weight plan that includes five feelings a day and one lean green meal daily. However, there are also other regimens of the Optavia Diet if the five fuelings a day is too much for you. And since this is a commercial diet, you have access to Optavia coaches and become part of a community that will encourage you to succeed in your weight loss journey. Moreover, this diet is also designed for people who want to transition from their old habits to healthier ones. Basically, this diet is not only for people who want to lose weight but also for people who suffer from diabetes, people suffering from gout, nursing moms, old as well as teens.

The Optavia Diet has been subjected to various studies to prove its efficacy in weight loss. Different studies were published in various journals indicating that those who follow this program are able to see significant changes in as little as 8 weeks and that people can achieve their long-term health goals with the Optavia Diet.

The Benefits of The Optavia Diet

The Optavia Diet, similar to other weight shedding programs, assures people a high success rate. However, unlike other programs, this particular diet program is not only easy to follow but it is also great for those who have long-term health goals. Thus, below are the benefits of following this diet regimen.

Structured Diet Plan: The Optavia diet has a structured diet plan, making it one of the most nutritious diets available. Everything is formulated for you, so you don't need to understand if you are following the diet correctly. As it is very easy to follow, it is ideal for people who are always busy or who do not have the ability to cook their food.

Ideal for Portion Controllers - One of the hardest parts of the diet is learning to control portions and stick to them. The Optavia diet is accompanied by the reload phase that helps keep your meals in check, so you don't need to eat unnecessarily.

Practice long-term relationship with food: Guiding the community to follow the Optavia diet can help improve a long-term positive relationship with food. Over time, you come to realize the types of foods you are allowed to eat and appreciate the healthy options you have.

No Responsibility Partner Needed: While some diets encourage you to make a friend to the diet, the Optavia diet is ideal for people who have no responsibility partners. The point is that people are connected to a community of dietitians who can provide the necessary support during the phases of this diet.

Better Overall Health - This particular diet is known to help improve overall well-being. In addition to weight loss, several studies have also shown that the Optavia diet can help people maintain blood sugar levels and stable blood pressure due to the limited sodium intake in food. In fact, Optavia provides less than 2,300 milligrams of sodium a day.

A Deeper Look into the Optavia Diet

The Optavia Diet encourages people to limit the number of calories that they should take daily. Under this program, dieters are encouraged to consume between 800 and 1000 calories daily. For this to be possible, dieters are encouraged to opt for healthier food items as well as meal replacements. But unlike other types of commercial diet regimens, the Optavia Diet comes in different variations. There are currently three variations of the Optavia Diet plan that one can choose from according to one's needs.

5&1 Optavia Diet Plan : This is the most common version of the Optavia Diet and it involves eating five prepackaged meals from the Optimal Health Fuelings and one home-made balanced meal.

4&2&1 Octavia Diet Plan: This diet plan is designed for people who want to have flexibility while following this regimen. Under this program, dieters are encouraged to eat more calories and have more flexible food choices. This means that they can consume 4 prepackaged Optimal Health Fuelings food, three home-cooked meals from the Lean and Green, and one snack daily.

5&2&2 Optavia Diet Plan: This diet plan is perfect for individuals who prefer to have a flexible meal plan in order to achieve a healthy weight. It is recommended for a wide variety of people. Under this diet regimen, dieters are required to eat 5 fuelings, 2 lean and green meals, and 2 healthy snacks.

3&3 Optavia Diet Plan: This particular Diet plan is created for people who have moderate weight problems and merely want to maintain a healthy body. Under this diet plan, dieters are encouraged to consume 3 prepackaged Optimal Health Fuelings and three home-cooked meals.

Optavia for Nursing Mothers : This diet regimen is designed for nursing mothers with babies of at least two months old. Aside from supporting breastfeeding mothers, it also encourages gradual weight loss.

Optavia for Diabetes : This Optavia Diet plan is designed for people who have Type 1 and Type 2 diabetes. The meal plans are designed so that dieters consume more green and lean meals depending on their needs and condition.

Optavia for Gout: This diet regimen incorporates a balance of foods that are low in purines and moderate in protein.

Optavia for old people (65 years and older) : Designed for seniors, this Optavia Diet plan has some variations following the components of Fuelings depending on the needs and activities of the senior dieters.

Optavia for Teen Boys and Optavia for Teen Girls (13-18 years old) : Designed for active teens, the Optavia for Teens Boys and Optavia for Teens Girls provide the right nutrition to growing teens.

Regardless of which type of Optavia Diet plan you choose, it is important that you talk with a coach to help you determine which plan is right for you based on your individual goals. This is to ensure that you get the most out of the plan that you have chosen.

How to Start This Diet

The Optavia Diet is comprised of different phases. A certified coach will educate you on the steps that you need to undertake if you want to follow this regimen. But for those who are new to this diet, here are some things to know, especially when first starting out on this diet.

Initial Steps

During this phase, people are encouraged to consume 800 to 1,000 calories to help you shed off at least 12 pounds within the next 12 weeks. For instance, if you are following the 5&1 Optavia Diet Plan, then you need to eat 1 meal every 2 or 3 hours and include a 30-minute moderate workout most days of your week. You need to consume not more than 100 grams of carbohydrates daily during this phase.

Further, consuming the Lean and Green meals are highly encouraged. It involves eating 7 ounces of cooked lean proteins and non-starchy vegetables of three servings, and two servings of healthy fats. This phase also encourages the dieter to include 1 optional snack per day such as ½ cup sugar-free gelatin, 3 celery sticks, and 12 ounces nuts. Aside from these things, below are other things that you need to remember when following this phase:

Make sure that the portion size recommendations are for cooked weight and not the raw weight of your ingredients

Opt for meals that are baked, grilled, broiled, or poached. Avoid frying foods as this will increase your calorie intake.

Eat at least two servings of fish rich in Omega-3 fatty acids. These include fishes like tuna, salmon, trout, mackerel, herring, and other cold-water fishes.

Choose meatless alternatives like tofu and tempeh.

Follow the program even when you are dining out. Keep in mind that drinking alcohol is discouraged when following this plan.

Maintenance Phase

As soon as you have achieved your target weight, the next phase is the transition stage. It is a 6-week stage that involves increasing your calorie intake to 1,550 per day. This is also the phase when you are allowed to add more varieties into your meal such as whole grains, low-fat dairy, and fruits.

After six weeks, you can now move into the 3&3 Optavia Diet plan, so you are required to eat three Lean and Green meals and 3 Fueling foods.

What can I eat and not eat?

There are lots of foods you can eat while on the Optavia diet. However, you need to know these foods by heart. This is especially true if you are new to this diet and need to strictly follow the 5 & 1 Optavia diet. Thus, this section is dedicated to the types of foods that you are allowed and not allowed to eat while following this diet regimen.

2

EXERCISE AND THE OPTAVIA DIET?

The group suggests 30 minutes of a moderate-intensity exercise similar to walking. Other activities that you can efficiently perform daily is suitable when you are on an Optavia diet. However, whatever exercise you decide to follow, make sure you start slowly and gradually increase the time and strength as your body allows. You will always run out of energy if you go overboard on the exercise. The Optimal Weight 5 & 1 package offers particular suggestions.

Pros and Cons of The Optavia Diet
Advantages of the Optavia Diet

Optavia's program could be an ideal choice for you if you want a clear and easy-to-follow meal plan that helps you lose weight quickly and provides integrated welfare support.

•Packaged Products Offer Convenience

The shakes, soups, and all other meal replacement products from Optavia are directly delivered to your door — a level of convenience not given by many other diets. Although you'll have to shop for your additives for "lean and green" recipes, Optavia's "fuelings" home delivery service saves time and effort. Once the items arrive, they make great 'grab-and-go' meals and are simple to process.

- Makes quick weight loss

Many healthy people need around 1600 to 3000 calories each day to keep their weight going. Besides, limiting the number to as low as 800 ensures that most people lose weight. Optavia's 5 & 1 strategy is meant for rapid weight loss, rendering it a reliable option to shed pounds on someone with a medical reason conveniently.

- Removes doubts

Many people find the most challenging part of dieting to be the mental effort required when figuring out what to eat every day — or even at every meal. Optavia soothes the burden of meal planning and "decision exhaustion" by offering users clear-cut accepted products with "fuelings" and "lean and green" menu recommendations.

- Provides Social Support

With any weight loss plan, social support is an essential determinant of success. The training program and group calls offered by Optavia offers built-in motivation and user support.

Disadvantages of the Optavia Diet

Optavia's plan also has potential downsides, specifically, if you're worried about cost, flexibility, and variety.

- High cost for the month

The cost of Optavia could be dissuasive to prospective users. The 5 & 1 strategy varies in price from $350 to $425 for 119 portions (about three weeks of meal substitutions). As you are comparing the cost of the program, don't forget to make a factor in the food you will have to buy to prepare your "lean and green" meals.

- Includes manufactured goods

While the "fuelings" of Optavia are manufactured with interchangeable nutrients, they are still undeniably processed foods. This is a turn-off for some consumers. Studies on nutrition have indicated that eating a lot of processed foods can have detrimental effects on one's wellbeing, so this part of the diet plan can be harmful.

•Loss of weight May is not permanent

One difficulty common to anybody on a diet is to decide how to sustain weight loss once the program is complete. The same applies to the Optavia system. When consumers go back to eating regular food instead of meal replacements from the program, they will notice that the weight they lose is recovered quickly.

•Calorie-restricting effects

While Optavia's diet plan emphasizes frequently eating throughout the day, each one of its "fuelings" offers just 110 calories. "Lean, nutritious" meals are low in calories, as well. In general, if you eat fewer calories, you might notice that the diet leaves you hungry and unsatisfied. You can feel more tired and even irritable, as well.

•Mealtime Sleep and Loneliness

The dependence of Optavia on meal replacements can interfere with the social aspects of food preparation and consumption. It may be uncomfortable or frustrating for consumers to have a shake or bar at family mealtime or when eating out with buddies.

3

HOW OPTAVIA DIET CAN HELP YOU

How Optavia Diet Can Help You Lose Weight

OPTAVIA diet plans are suitable for all persons regardless of current age or weight. However, such factors will determine how long you will continue using the diet plan. Current age, weight, and overall health will also determine how well a person conforms to the dietary program.

The 2017 report funded by Medifast discovered that more than 70 percent of overweight adults who were placed on Medifast and received one-on-one behavioral support lost more than 5 percent of their body mass.

Following the Diet Plan

With the OPTAVIA diet plan, you will enjoy more than 60 Fueling options. However, you will find it difficult to stop going on that diet. Also, you would get to take in more Optavia meal every time without taking sock of what you are consuming. This is because there are no sugars, points, or calories to record.

More studies showed that sticking to the Optavia diet plan is easy compared to other regular eating regimens. According to a 2008 study published in the Diabetes Educator, 16 out of 119

Medifast dietitians completed the eating regimen in 86 weeks. In contrast, only eight out of the 119 participants that tried regular diets were able to continue for 86 weeks.

Recipes are available on different online platforms. Besides, it is possible to have a complete Optavia meal for dinner. It is fast and cheap to order meals and cook them. Adherents can also depend on their OPTAVIA instructors and online forums for knowledge and techniques.

The official Pinterest page of Optavia is an excellent example of where beginners can get some tips on the best lean and green meals. You can use the page as a conversion recipe guide to help you incorporate their ideas into your cooking plans.

Eating an all-out Optavia diet may be tough, but it is possible. The diet creators, Medifast group, recommend that you make a lean and green lunch for a day. There are tips and ideas on how to go about this on the company's official webpage. The guide available on the page offers tips for selecting drinks and picking toppings with condiments. For example, ask for your steak (not more than 7-ounce) to be provided without herbal butter and replace the baked potato with steamed broccoli.

Picking an eating regimen and making orders is very easy. Medifast group offers automatic delivery. The only difficulty that will be experienced when cooking OPTAVIA meals involves the addition of water and microwave nuking. Any random person or regular cook should be able to make a lean and green meal without much stress.

Medifast also states its diets have a healthy "fullness" level. This means that you can stay satisfied for a long time because of the high fiber and protein content. A 2010 report published in the Nutrition Journal observed that there are no significant discrepancies in satiety in post-meal or general fullness between the Optavia diet and other eating plans. The research on Diabetes Educator also found no significant association in dietary appetite across different types of diet. This is very important as specialists in nutrition have emphasized the relationship between satiety (the satisfying feeling you've had enough) and dietary plans.

Optavia diet from Medifast is ideal as the creators reveal that a panel tastes all their services before putting it on the market for their customers. The company also carries out different tracking of customer feedback regularly. Although this will not necessarily make the diet better than other dietary brands, the company believes it will satisfy their customers. OPTAVIA Fuelings do not involve artificial colors, sweeteners, or flavors.

4

POSSIBLE DOWNSIDES OF THE OPTAVIA DIET

Although the Optavia diet is an effective weight-loss tool, it has some potential disadvantages. Some of its downsides are:

Meager calorie consumption

The Optavia diet only room for only 800-1,200 calories consumed daily while on the 5&1 plan, which is very low for an adult consuming more than 2,000 calories before then.

Even though the low-calorie intake can significantly result in weight loss, it can also lead to muscle loss.

Studies have shown that low-calorie diets can lead to frequent hunger and cravings, which can make adhering to the diet plan more difficult.

It can be challenging to stick with

The 5&1 plan of the Optavia diet program includes 5 prepackaged fuelings and 1 Lean and Green meal (low carb) only. This shows that the program has restricted food options and low-calorie count; hence, it can be difficult to stick by it.

Since the food options are restricted and not what you are used to, you can get tired along the line while on the program, and as such, you can easily develop cravings for other foods and cheat on the diet.

Even though the maintenance plan is not as restrictive as the other 2 control plans, it also depends mainly on fuelings.

The Optavia Diet program can be Expensive.

The Optavia diet can be costly regardless of which of the plan you chose.

An average of 3 weeks' worth of Optavia fuelings, which can be in the region of 120 servings while on the 5&1 plan can cost between $350-$450. However, this cost will also include the coaching for that period, but it does not cover the cost of groceries for the recommended Lean and Green meals.

How Nutritious is Optavia Diet

Below is the breakdown comparison of the nutritional content of meals on the Optavial Weight 5&1 Plan and the federal government's 2015 Dietary Guidelines for Americans.

Note that since lean and green meals vary, the figures given below are estimates. The diet figures are retrieved from OPTAVIA:

Optimal Weight 5&1 Plan
Federal Government Recommendation
Calories
800-1,000
Men
19-25: 2,800
26-45: 2,600
46-65: 2,400
65+: 2,200
Women
19-25: 2,200
26-50: 2,000
51+: 1,800
Total fat
% of Calorie Intake
20%
20%-35%

Saturated Fat
% of Calorie Intake
3%-5%
Less than 10%
Trans Fat
% of Calorie Intake
0%
N/A
Total Carbohydrates
% of Calorie Intake
40%
45%-65%
Sugars
(Total except as noted)
10%-20%
N/A
Fiber
25 g – 30 g
Men
19-30: 34 g.
31-50: 31 g.
51+: 28 g.
Women
19-30: 28 g.
31-50: 25 g.
51+: 22 g.
Protein
% of Calorie Intake
40%
10%-35%
Sodium
Under 2,300 mg
Under 2,300 mg.
Potassium
Average 3,000 mg
At least 4,700 mg.

Calcium
1,000 mg – 1,200 mg
Men
1,000 mg.
Women
19-50: 1,000 mg.
51+: 1,200 mg.
Vitamin B-12
2.4 mcg
2.4 mcg.
Vitamin D
20 mcg – 50 mcg.
15 mcg

Note that: g = gram, mg = milligram, mcg = microgram

Do's & Don'ts of the Optavia Diet

The Optavia diet plan has some guidelines, especially in food consumption that must be adhered to if you wish to record a significant success with the diet plan.

Recommended Foods to Eat

The foods you are allowed to eat while on the 5&1 plan are the 5 Optavia fuellings and 1 Lean and Green meal daily.

The meals consist mainly of healthy fats, lean protein, and low carb vegetables, and there is a recommendation for only 2 servings of fatty fish every week. Some beverages and low carb condiments are also allowed in small proportions.

The foods that are Allowed

✓ Fish and Shellfish: Trout, tuna, halibut, salmon, crab, scallops, lobster, shrimp.

✓ Meat: Lean beef, lamb, chicken, game meats, turkey, tenderloin or pork chop, ground meat (must be 85% lean at least)

✓ Vegetable oils: walnut, flaxseed, olive oil, and canola

✓ Eggs: Whole eggs, egg beaters, egg whites

✓ Additional healthy fats: reduced-fat margarine, walnuts, pistachios, almonds, avocado, olives, low carb salad dressings.

✓ Soy Products: Tofu

✓ Sugar-free beverages: unsweetened almond milk, coffee, tea, water

✓ Sugar-free snacks: gelatin, mints, popsicles, gum

✓ Low carb vegetables: celery, mushrooms, cauliflower, zucchini, peppers, jicama, spinach, cucumbers, cabbage, eggplant, broccoli, spaghetti squash, collard greens

✓ Seasonings and Condiments: lemon juice, yellow mustard, salsa, zero-calorie sweeteners, barbecue sauce, cocktail sauce, dried herbs, salt, spices, lime juice, soy sauce, sugar-free syrup, teaspoons only of ketchup.

Foods that are not Allowed

Apart from the carbs contained in the prepackaged Optavia fuelings, most carb-containing beverages and foods are not allowed while you are on the 5&1 Plan. Some fats are also banned as well as all fried foods.

Below are the foods you must avoid except they are included in your fuelings:

✓ Refined grains: pasta, pancakes, crackers, cookies, pastries, white bread, biscuits, flour tortillas, white rice, cakes

✓ Fried foods: Fish, vegetables, shellfish, meats, sweets like pastries

✓ Whole fat dairy: cheese, milk, yogurt

✓ Certain fats: coconut oil, butter, solid shortening

✓ Sugar-sweetened beverages: fruit juice, soda, energy drinks, sports drinks, sweet tea

✓ Alcohol: All varieties

The foods below are banned while on the 5&1 plan but are added for the 6-week transition phase and with no restriction during the 3&3 Plan:

✓ Fruit: All fresh fruit

✓ Whole grains: high fiber breakfast cereal, whole grain bread, whole-wheat pasta, brown rice

✓ Starch vegetables: corn, white potatoes, sweet potatoes, peas

✓ Low-fat or fat-free dairy: milk, yogurt, cheese

✓ Legumes: Beans, peas, lentils, soybeans

Note that during the 6 weeks' transition phase, and while on the 3&3 plan, you are advised to eat more berries if you must take fruits as they contain lower carbs.

Summary: *You will need to avoid sugar-sweetened beverages, refined grains, fried food, and alcohol while on the Optavia diet. However, during the transition and maintenance phases, some of the restrictions are relaxed, and some carb-containing foods are introduced like fresh fruit and low-fat dairy.*

LEAN AND GREEN RECIPES (BREAKFAST)

1

TASTY BREAKFAST DONUTS

Preparation Time: 5 minutes
Cooking Time: 5 minutes
Servings: 4
Ingredients:
43 grams' cream cheese
2 eggs
2 tablespoons almond flour
2 tablespoons erythritol
1 ½ tablespoons coconut flour
½ teaspoon baking powder
½ teaspoon vanilla extract
5 drops Stevia (liquid form)
2 strips bacon, fried until crispy

Directions:
Rub coconut oil over donut maker and turn on.

Pulse all ingredients except bacon in a blender or food processor until smooth (should take around 1 minute).

Pour batter into donut maker, leaving 1/10 in each round for rising.

Leave for 3 minutes before flipping each donut. Leave for

another 2 minutes or until the fork comes out clean when piercing them.

Take donuts out and let cool.

Repeat steps 1-5 until all batter is used.

Crumble bacon into bits and use to top donuts.

Nutrition:

Calories: 60

Fat: 5g

Carbs: 1g

Fiber: 0g

Protein: 3g

2
CHEESY SPICY BACON BOWLS

Preparation Time: 10 minutes
Cooking Time: 22 minutes
Servings: 12
Ingredients:
6 strips Bacon, pan fried until cooked but still malleable
4 eggs
60 grams' cheddar cheese
40 grams' cream cheese, grated
2 Jalapenos, sliced and seeds removed
2 tablespoons coconut oil
¼ teaspoon onion powder
¼ teaspoon garlic powder
Dash of salt and pepper
Directions:
Preheat oven to 375 degrees Fahrenheit

In a bowl, beat together eggs, cream cheese, jalapenos (minus 6 slices), coconut oil, onion powder, garlic powder, and salt and pepper.

Using leftover bacon grease on a muffin tray, rubbing it into each insert. Place bacon wrapped inside the parameters of each insert.

Pour beaten mixture half way up each bacon bowl.

Garnish each bacon bowl with cheese and leftover jalapeno slices (placing one on top of each).

Leave in the oven for about 22 minutes, or until egg is thoroughly cooked and cheese is bubbly.

Remove from oven and let cool until edible.

Enjoy!

Nutrition:
Calories: 259
Fat: 24g
Carbs: 1g
Fiber: 0g
Protein: 10g

3
GOAT CHEESE ZUCCHINI KALE QUICHE

Preparation Time: 35 minutes
Cooking Time: 1 hour 10 minutes
Servings: 4
Ingredients:
4 large eggs
8 ounces' fresh zucchini, sliced
10 ounces' kale
3 garlic cloves (minced)
1 cup of soy milk
1 ounce's goat cheese
1 cup grated parmesan
1 cup shredded cheddar cheese
2 teaspoons olive oil
Salt & pepper, to taste
Directions:
Preheat oven to 350°F.
Heat 1 tsp of olive oil in a saucepan over medium-high heat. Sauté garlic for 1 minute until flavored.
Add the zucchini and cook for another 5-7 minutes until soft.
Beat the eggs and then add a little milk and Parmesan cheese.

Meanwhile, heat the remaining olive oil in another saucepan and add the cabbage. Cover and cook for 5 minutes until dry.

Slightly grease a baking dish with cooking spray and spread the kale leaves across the bottom. Add the zucchini and top with goat cheese.

Pour the egg, milk and parmesan mixture evenly over the other ingredients. Top with cheddar cheese.

Bake for 50–60 minutes until golden brown. Check the center of the quiche, it should have a solid consistency.

Let chill for a few minutes before serving.

Nutrition:
Total Carbohydrates: 15g
Dietary Fiber: 2g
Net Carbs: 13g
Protein: 19g
Total Fat: 18g
Calories: 290

4

CREAM CHEESE EGG BREAKFAST

Preparation Time: 5 minutes
Cooking Time: 5 minutes
Servings: 4
Ingredients:
2 eggs, beaten
1 tablespoon butter
2 tablespoons soft cream cheese with chives
Directions:
Melt the butter in a small skillet. Add the eggs and cream cheese. Stir and cook to desired doneness.
Nutrition:
Calories: 341
Fat: 31g
Protein: 15g
Carbohydrate: 0g
Dietary Fiber: 3g

5

AVOCADO RED PEPPERS ROASTED SCRAMBLED EGGS

Preparation Time: 10 minutes
Cooking Time: 12 minutes
Servings: 3
Ingredients:
1/2 tablespoon butter
Eggs, 2
1/2 roasted red pepper, about 1 1/2 ounces
1/2 small avocado, coarsely chopped, about 2 1/4 ounces
Salt, to taste

Directions:
In a nonstick skillet, heat the butter over medium heat. Break the eggs into the pan and break the yolks with a spoon. Sprinkle with a little salt.

Stir to stir and continue stirring until the eggs start to come out. Quickly add the bell peppers and avocado.

Cook and stir until the eggs suit your taste. Adjust the seasoning, if necessary.

Nutrition:
Calories: 317

Fat: 26g
Protein: 14g
Dietary Fiber: 5g
Net Carbs: 4g

6

MUSHROOM QUICKIE SCRAMBLE

Preparation Time: 10 minutes
Cooking Time: 10 minutes
Servings: 4
Ingredients:
3 small sized eggs, whisked
4 pcs. bella mushrooms
½ cup of spinach
¼ cup of red bell peppers
2 deli ham slices
1 tablespoon of ghee or coconut oil
Salt & pepper to taste
Directions:
Chop the ham and veggies.
Put half a tbsp of butter in a frying pan and heat until melted.
Sauté the ham and vegetables in a frying pan then set aside.
Get a new frying pan and heat the remaining butter.
Add the whisked eggs into the second pan while stirring continuously to avoid overcooking.
When the eggs are done, sprinkle with salt & pepper to taste.
Add the ham and veggies to the pan with the eggs.

Mix well.

Remove from burner and transfer to a plate.

Serve and enjoy.

Nutrition:

Calories: 350

Total Fat: 29 g

Protein: 21 g

Total Carbs: 5

7

COCONUT COFFEE AND GHEE

Preparation Time: 10 minutes
Cooking Time: 10 minutes
Servings: 5
Ingredients:
½ Tbsp. of coconut oil
½ Tbsp. of ghee
1 to 2 cups of preferred coffee (or rooibos or black tea, if preferred)
1 Tbsp. of coconut or almond milk
Directions:
Place the almond (or coconut) milk, coconut oil, ghee and coffee in a blender (or milk frothier).
mix for around 10 seconds or until the coffee turns creamy and foamy.
Pour contents into a coffee cup.
Serve immediately and enjoy.
Nutrition:
Calories: 150
Total Fat: 15 g

Protein: 0 g
Total Carbs: 0 g
Net Carbs: 0 g

8

YUMMY VEGGIE WAFFLES

Preparation Time: 10 minutes
Cooking Time: 9 minutes
Servings: 3
Ingredients:
3 cups raw cauliflower, grated
1 cup cheddar cheese
1 cup mozzarella cheese
½ cup parmesan
1/3 cup chives, finely sliced
6 eggs
1 teaspoon garlic powder
1 teaspoon onion powder
½ teaspoon chili flakes
Dash of salt and pepper

Directions:
Turn waffle maker on.

In a bowl mix all the listed ingredients very well until incorporated.

Once waffle maker is hot, distribute waffle mixture into the insert.

Let cook for about 9 minutes, flipping at 6 minutes.

Remove from waffle maker and set aside.

Repeat the previous steps with the rest of the batter until gone (should come out to 4 waffles)

Serve and enjoy!

Nutrition:

Calories: 390

Fat: 28g

Carbs: 6g

Fiber: 2g

Protein: 30g

9

OMEGA 3 BREAKFAST SHAKE

Preparation Time: 5 minutes
Cooking Time: 5 minutes
Servings: 2
Ingredients:
1 cup vanilla almond milk (unsweetened)
2 tablespoons blueberries
1 ½ tablespoons flaxseed meal
1 tablespoon MCT Oil
¾ tablespoon banana extract
½ tablespoon chia seeds
5 drops Stevia (liquid form)
1/8 tablespoon Xanthan gum

Directions:

In a blender, pulse vanilla almond milk, banana extract, Stevia, and 3 ice cubes.

When smooth, add blueberries and pulse.

Once blueberries are thoroughly incorporated, add flaxseed meal and chia seeds.

Let sit for 5 minutes.

After 5 minutes, pulse again until all ingredients are nicely distributed. Serve and enjoy

Nutrition:
Calories: 264
Fats: 25g
Carbs: 7g
Protein: 4g

10
BACON SPAGHETTI SQUASH CARBONARA

Preparation Time: 20 minutes
Cooking Time: 40 minutes
Servings: 4
Ingredients:
1 small spaghetti squash
6 ounces' bacon (roughly chopped)
1 large tomato (sliced)
2 chives (chopped)
1 garlic clove (minced)
6 ounces' low-fat cottage cheese
1 cup Gouda cheese (grated)
2 tablespoons olive oil
Salt and pepper, to taste
Directions:
Preheat the oven to 350°F.

Cut the squash spaghetti in half, brush with some olive oil and bake for 20–30 minutes, skin side up. Remove from the oven and remove the core with a fork, creating the spaghetti.

Heat one tablespoon of olive oil in a skillet. Cook the bacon for about 1 minute until crispy.

Quickly wipe out the pan with paper towels.

Heat another tablespoon of oil and sauté the garlic, tomato and chives for 2–3 minutes. Add the spaghetti and sauté for another 5 minutes, stirring occasionally to keep from burning.

Begin to add the cottage cheese, about 2 tablespoons at a time. If the sauce becomes thicken, add about a cup of water. The sauce should be creamy, but not too runny or thick. Allow to cook for another 3 minutes.

Serve immediately.

Nutrition:
Calories: 305
Total Fat: 21g
Net Carbs: 8g
Protein: 18g

11

LIME BACON THYME MUFFINS

Preparation Time: 10 minutes
Cooking Time: 20 minutes
Servings: 3
Ingredients:
3 cups of almond flour
4 medium-sized eggs
1 cup of bacon bits
2 tsp. of lemon thyme
½ cup of melted ghee
1 tsp. of baking soda
½ tsp. of salt, to taste

Directions:
Pre-heat oven to 3500 F.
Put ghee in mixing bowl and melt.
Add baking soda and almond flour.
Put the eggs in.
Add the lemon thyme (if preferred, other herbs or spices may be used).
Drizzle with salt.
Mix all ingredients well.

Sprinkle with bacon bits

Line the muffin pan with liners.

Spoon mixture into the pan, filling the pan to about ¾ full.

Bake for about 20 minutes. Test by inserting a toothpick into a muffin. If it comes out clean, then the muffins are done.

Serve immediately.

Nutrition:

Calories: 300

Total Fat: 28 g

Protein: 11 g

Total Carbs: 6 g

Fiber: 3 g

12

GLUTEN-FREE PANCAKES

Preparation Time: 5 minutes
Cooking Time: 2 minutes
Servings: 2
Ingredients:
6 eggs
1 cup low-fat cream cheese
1 1/12; teaspoons baking powder
1 scoop protein powder
1/4; cup almond meal
¼ teaspoon salt

Directions:

Combine dry ingredients in a food processor. Add the eggs one after another and then the cream cheese. Edit until you have a blast.

Lightly grease a skillet with cooking spray and place over medium-high heat.

Pour the batter into the pan. Turn the pan gently to create round pancakes.

Cook for about 2 minutes on each side.

Serve pancakes with your favorite topping.

Nutrition:
Dietary Fiber: 1g
Net Carbs: 5g
Protein: 25g
Total Fat: 14g
Calories: 288

13

MUSHROOM & SPINACH OMELET

Preparation Time: 20 minutes
Cooking Time: 20 minutes
Servings: 3
Ingredients:
2 tablespoons butter, divided
6-8 fresh mushrooms, sliced, 5 ounces
Chives, chopped, optional
Salt and pepper, to taste
1 handful baby spinach, about 1/2 ounce
Pinch garlic powder
4 eggs, beaten
1-ounce shredded Swiss cheese,

Directions:

In a very large saucepan, sauté the mushrooms in 1 tablespoon of butter until soft. season with salt, pepper and garlic.

Remove the mushrooms from the pan and keep warm. Heat the remaining tablespoon of butter in the same skillet over medium heat.

Beat the eggs with a little salt and pepper and add to the hot butter. Turn the pan over to coat the entire bottom of the pan with egg. Once the egg is almost out, place the cheese over the middle of the tortilla.

Fill the cheese with spinach leaves and hot mushrooms. Let cook for about a minute for the spinach to start to wilt. Fold the empty side of the tortilla carefully over the filling and slide it onto a plate and sprinkle with chives, if desired.

Alternatively, you can make two tortillas using half the mushroom, spinach, and cheese filling in each.

Nutrition:
Calories: 321
Fat: 26g
Protein: 19g
Carbohydrate: 4g
Dietary Fiber: 1g

LEAN AND GREEN RECIPES (LUNCH)

14

TOMATILLO AND GREEN CHILI PORK STEW

Preparation Time: 10 minutes
Cooking Time: 20 minutes
Servings: 4
Ingredients:
2 scallions, chopped
2 cloves of garlic
1 lb. tomatillos, trimmed and chopped
8 large romaine or green lettuce leaves, divided
2 serrano chilies, seeds, and membranes
½ tsp of dried Mexican oregano (or you can use regular oregano)
1 ½ lb. of boneless pork loin, to be cut into bite-sized cubes
¼ cup of cilantro, chopped
¼ tablespoon (each) salt and paper
1 jalapeno, seeds and membranes to be removed and thinly sliced
1 cup of sliced radishes
4 lime wedges
Directions:

Combine scallions, garlic, tomatillos, 4 lettuce leaves, serrano chilies, and oregano in a blender. Then puree until smooth

Put pork and tomatillo mixture in a medium pot. 1-inch of puree should cover the pork; if not, add water until it covers it. Season with pepper & salt, and cover it simmers. Simmer on heat for approximately 20 minutes.

Now, finely shred the remaining lettuce leaves.

When the stew is done cooking, garnish with cilantro, radishes, finely shredded lettuce, sliced jalapenos, and lime wedges.

Nutrition:
Calories: 370
Protein: 36g
Carbohydrate: 14g
Fat: 19 g

15

OPTAVIA CLOUD BREAD

Preparation Time: 25 minutes
Cooking Time: 35 minutes
Servings: 3

Ingredients:

½ cup of Fat-free 0% Plain Greek Yogurt (4.4 0z)
3 Eggs, Separated
16 teaspoon Cream of Tartar
1 Packet sweetener (a granulated sweetener just like stevia)

Directions:

For about 30 minutes before making this meal, place the Kitchen Aid Bowl and the whisk attachment in the freezer.

Preheat your oven to 30 degrees

Remove the mixing bowl and whisk attachment from the freezer

Separate the eggs. Now put the egg whites in the Kitchen Aid Bowl, and they should be in a different medium-sized bowl.

In the medium-sized bowl containing the yolks, mix in the sweetener and yogurt.

In the bowl containing the egg white, add in the cream of tartar. Beat this mixture until the egg whites turn to stiff peaks.

Now, take the egg yolk mixture and carefully fold it into the egg whites. Be cautious and avoid over-stirring.

Place baking paper on a baking tray and spray with cooking spray.

Scoop out 6 equally-sized "blobs" of the "dough" onto the parchment paper.

Bake for about 25-35 minutes (make sure you check when it is 25 minutes, in some ovens, they are done at this timestamp). You will know they are done as they will get brownish at the top and have some crack.

Most people like them cold against being warm

Most people like to re-heat in a toast oven or toaster to get them a little bit crispy.

Your serving size should be about 2 pieces.

Nutrition:
Calories: 234
Protein: 23g
Carbs: 5g
Fiber: 8g
Sodium: 223g

16

AVOCADO LIME SHRIMP SALAD

Preparation Time: 15 minutes
Cooking Time: 0 minutes
Servings: 2
Ingredients:

14 ounces of jumbo cooked shrimp, peeled and deveined; chopped

4 ½ ounces of avocado, diced

1 ½ cup of tomato, diced

¼ cup of chopped green onion

¼ cup of jalapeno with the seeds removed, diced fine

1 teaspoon of olive oil

2 tablespoons of lime juice

1/8 teaspoon of salt

1 tablespoon of chopped cilantro

Directions:

Get a small bowl and combine green onion, olive oil, lime juice, pepper, a pinch of salt. Wait for about 5 minutes for all of them to marinate and mellow the flavor of the onion.

Get a large bowl and combined chopped shrimp, tomato,

avocado, jalapeno. Combine all of the ingredients, add cilantro, and gently toss.

Add pepper and salt as desired.

Nutrition:
Calories: 314
Protein: 26g
Carbs: 15g
Fiber: 9g

17

BROCCOLI CHEDDAR BREAKFAST BAKE

Preparation Time: 10 minutes
Cooking Time: 45 minutes
Servings: 4
Ingredients:
9 eggs
6 cups of small broccoli florets
¼ teaspoon of salt
1 cup of unsweetened almond milk
¼ teaspoon of cayenne pepper
¼ teaspoon of ground pepper
Cooking spray
4 oz. of shredded, reduced-fat cheddar
Directions:
Preheat your oven to about 375 degrees

In your large microwave-safe, add broccoli and 2 to 3 tablespoon of water. Microwave on high heat for 4 minutes or until it becomes tender. Now transfer the broccoli to a colander to drain excess liquid

Get a medium-sized bowl and whisk the milk, eggs, and seasonings together.

Set the broccoli neatly on the bottom of a lightly greased 13 x 9-inch baking dish. Sprinkle the cheese gently on the broccoli and pour the egg mixture on top of it.

Bake for about 45 minutes or until the center is set and the top forms a light brown crust.

Nutrition:
Calories: 290
Protein: 25g
Carbohydrate: 8g
Fat: 18 g

18

GRILLED MAHI MAHI WITH JICAMA SLAW

Preparation Time: 20 minutes
Cooking Time: 10 minutes
Servings: 4
Ingredients:
1 teaspoon each for pepper and salt, divided
1 tablespoon of lime juice, divided
2 tablespoon + 2 teaspoons of extra virgin olive oil
4 raw mahi-mahi fillets, which should be about 8 oz. each
½ cucumber which should be thinly cut into long strips like matchsticks (it should yield about 1 cup)
1 jicama, which should be thinly cut into long strips like matchsticks (it should yield about 3 cups)
1 cup of alfalfa sprouts
2 cups of coarsely chopped watercress

Directions:
Combine ½ teaspoon of both pepper and salt, 1 teaspoon of lime juice, and 2 teaspoons of oil in a small bowl. Then brush the mahi-mahi fillets all through with the olive oil mixture.

Grill the mahi-mahi on medium-high heat until it becomes done in about 5 minutes, turn it to the other side, and let it be done for about 5 minutes. (You will have an internal temperature of about 1450F).

For the slaw, combine the watercress, cucumber, jicama, and alfalfa sprouts in a bowl. Now combine ½ teaspoon of both pepper and salt, 2 teaspoons of lime juice, and 2 tablespoons of extra virgin oil in a small bowl. Drizzle it over slaw and toss together to combine.

Nutrition:
Calories: 320
Protein: 44g
Carbohydrate: 10g
Fat: 11 g

19

ROSEMARY CAULIFLOWER ROLLS

Preparation Time: 10 minutes
Cooking Time: 30 minutes
Servings: 3
Ingredients:
1/3 cup of almond flour
4 cups of riced cauliflower
1/3 cup of reduced-fat, shredded mozzarella or cheddar cheese
2 eggs
2 tablespoon of fresh rosemary, finely chopped
½ teaspoon of salt
Directions:
Preheat your oven to 4000F
Combine all the listed ingredients in a medium-sized bowl
Scoop cauliflower mixture into 12 evenly-sized rolls/biscuits onto a lightly-greased and foil-lined baking sheet.
Bake until it turns golden brown, which should be achieved in about 30 minutes.
Note: if you want to have the outside of the rolls/biscuits crisp, then broil for some minutes before serving.

Nutrition:
Calories: 254
Protein: 24g
Carbohydrate: 7g
Fat: 8 g

20

MEDITERRANEAN CHICKEN SALAD

Preparation Time: 5 minutes
Cooking Time: 25 minutes
Servings: 4
Ingredients:
For Chicken:
1 ¾ lb. boneless, skinless chicken breast
¼ teaspoon each of pepper and salt (or as desired)
1 ½ tablespoon of butter, melted
For Mediterranean salad:
1 cup of sliced cucumber
6 cups of romaine lettuce, that is torn or roughly chopped
10 pitted Kalamata olives
1 pint of cherry tomatoes
1/3 cup of reduced-fat feta cheese
¼ teaspoon each of pepper and salt (or lesser)
1 small lemon juice (it should be about 2 tablespoons)
Directions:
Preheat your oven or grill to about 3500F.
Season the chicken with salt, butter, and black pepper
Roast or grill chicken until it reaches an internal temperature

of 1650F in about 25 minutes. Once your chicken breasts are cooked, remove and keep aside to rest for about 5 minutes before you slice it.

Combine all the salad ingredients you have and toss everything together very well

Serve the chicken with Mediterranean salad

Nutrition:
Calories: 340
Protein: 45g
Carbohydrate: 9g
Fat: 4 g

LEAN AND GREEN RECIPES (DINNER) MEAT AND FISH

21

CHIPOTLE CHICKEN & CAULIFLOWER RICE BOWLS

Preparation Time: 10 minutes
Cooking Time: 20 minutes
Servings: 4
Ingredients:
1/3 cup of salsa
1 quantity of 14.5 oz. of can fire-roasted diced tomatoes
1 canned chipotle pepper + 1 teaspoon sauce
½ teaspoon of dried oregano
1 teaspoon of cumin
1 ½ lb. of boneless, skinless chicken breast
¼ teaspoon of salt
1 cup of reduced-fat shredded Mexican cheese blend
4 cups of frozen riced cauliflower
½ medium-sized avocado, sliced

Directions:
Combine the first ingredients in a blender and blend until they become smooth

Place chicken inside your instant pot, and pour the sauce over it. Cover the lid and close the pressure valve. Set it to 20 minutes at high temperature. Let the pressure release on its own before opening. Remove the piece and the chicken and then add it back to the sauce.

Microwave the riced cauliflower according to the directions on the package

Before you serve, divide the riced cauliflower, cheese, avocado, and chicken equally among the 4 bowls.

Nutrition:

Calories: 287

Protein: 35g

Carbohydrate: 19g

Fat: 12 g

22

LEMON GARLIC OREGANO CHICKEN WITH ASPARAGUS

Preparation Time: 5 minutes
Cooking Time: 40 minutes
Servings: 4
Ingredients:
1 small lemon, juiced (this should be about 2 tablespoons of lemon juice)
1 ¾ lb. of bone-in, skinless chicken thighs
2 tablespoon of fresh oregano, minced
2 cloves of garlic, minced
2 lbs. of asparagus, trimmed
¼ teaspoon each or less for black pepper and salt
Directions:
Preheat the oven to about 3500F.

Put the chicken in a medium-sized bowl. Now, add the garlic, oregano, lemon juice, pepper, and salt and toss together to combine.

Roast the chicken in the airfryer oven until it reaches an internal temperature of 1650F in about 40 minutes. Once the chicken thighs have been cooked, remove and keep aside to rest.

Now, steam the asparagus on a stovetop or in a microwave to the desired doneness.

Serve asparagus with the roasted chicken thighs.

Nutrition:

Calories: 350
Fat: 10 g
Carbohydrate: 10 g
Protein: 32 g

23

SHEET PAN CHICKEN FAJITA LETTUCE WRAPS

Preparation Time: 15 minutes
Cooking Time: 30 minutes
Servings: 2
Ingredients:
1 lb. chicken breast, thinly sliced into strips
2 teaspoon of olive oil
2 bell peppers, thinly sliced into strips
2 teaspoon of fajita seasoning
6 leaves from a romaine heart
Juice of half a lime
¼ cup plain of non-fat Greek yogurt
Directions:
Preheat your oven to about 4000F

Combine all of the ingredients except for lettuce in a large plastic bag that can be resealed. Mix very well to coat vegetables and chicken with oil and seasoning evenly.

Spread the contents of the bag evenly on a foil-lined baking sheet. Bake it for about 25-30 minutes, until the chicken is thoroughly cooked.

Serve on lettuce leaves and topped with Greek yogurt if you like

Nutrition:
Calories: 387
Fat: 6 g
Carbohydrate: 14 g
Protein: 18 g

24

SAVORY CILANTRO SALMON

Preparation Time: 10 minutes
Cooking Time: 30 minutes
Servings: 4
Ingredients:
2 tablespoons of fresh lime or lemon
4 cups of fresh cilantro, divided
2 tablespoon of hot red pepper sauce
½ teaspoon of salt. Divided
1 teaspoon of cumin
4, 7 oz. of salmon filets
½ cup of (4 oz.) water
2 cups of sliced red bell pepper
2 cups of sliced yellow bell pepper
2 cups of sliced green bell pepper
Cooking spray
½ teaspoon of pepper
Directions:
Get a blender or food processor and combine half of the cilantro, lime juice or lemon, cumin, hot red pepper sauce, water,

and salt; then puree until they become smooth. Transfer the marinade gotten into a large re-sealable plastic bag.

Add salmon to marinade. Seal the bag, squeeze out air that might have been trapped inside, turn to coat salmon. Refrigerate for about 1 hour, turning as often as possible.

Now, after marinating, preheat your oven to about 4000F. Arrange the pepper slices in a single layer in a slightly-greased, medium-sized square baking dish. Bake it for 20 minutes, turn the pepper slices once.

Drain your salmon and do away with the marinade. Crust the upper part of the salmon with the remaining chopped, fresh cilantro. Place salmon on the top of the pepper slices and bake for about 12-14 minutes until you observe that the fish flakes easily when it is being tested with a fork

Enjoy

Nutrition:

Calories: 350

Carbohydrate: 15 g

Protein: 42 g

Fat: 13 g

25

SALMON FLORENTINE

Preparation Time: 5 minutes
Cooking Time: 30 minutes
Servings: 4
Ingredients:
1 ½ cups of chopped cherry tomatoes
½ cup of chopped green onions
2 garlic cloves, minced
1 teaspoon of olive oil
1 quantity of 12 oz. package frozen chopped spinach, thawed and patted dry
¼ teaspoon of crushed red pepper flakes
½ cup of part-skim ricotta cheese
¼ teaspoon each for pepper and salt
4 quantities of 5 ½ oz. wild salmon fillets
Cooking spray
Directions:
Preheat the oven to 3500F

Get a medium skillet to cook onions in oil until they start to soften, which should be in about 2 minutes. You can then add garlic inside the skillet and cook for an extra 1 minute. Add the spinach, red pepper flakes, tomatoes, pepper, and salt. Cook for 2 minutes while stirring. Remove the pan from the heat and let it cool for about 10 minutes. Stir in the ricotta

Put a quarter of the spinach mixture on top of each salmon fillet. Place the fillets on a slightly-greased rimmed baking sheet and bake it for 15 minutes or until you are sure that the salmon has been thoroughly cooked.

Nutrition:

Calories: 350

Carbohydrate: 15 g

Protein: 42 g

Fat: 13 g

26

TOMATO BRAISED CAULIFLOWER WITH CHICKEN

Preparation Time: 10 minutes
Cooking Time: 30 minutes
Servings: 4
Ingredients:
4 garlic cloves, sliced
3 scallions, to be trimmed and cut into 1-inch pieces
¼ teaspoon of dried oregano
¼ teaspoon of crushed red pepper flakes
4 ½ cups of cauliflower
1 ½ cups of diced canned tomatoes
1 cup of fresh basil, gently torn
½ teaspoon each of pepper and salt, divided
1 ½ teaspoon of olive oil
1 ½ lb. of boneless, skinless chicken breasts
Directions:
Get a saucepan and combine the garlic, scallions, oregano, crushed red pepper, cauliflower, and tomato, and add ¼ cup of water. Get everything boil together and add ¼ teaspoon of pepper and salt for seasoning, then cover the pot with a lid. Let it simmer for 10 minutes and stir as often as possible until you

observe that the cauliflower is tender. Now, wrap up the seasoning with the remaining ¼ teaspoon of pepper and salt.

Toss the chicken breast with oil, olive prefebrably and let it roast in the oven with the heat of 4500F for 20 minutes and an internal temperature of 1650F. Allow the chicken to rest for like 10 minutes.

Now slice the chicken, and serve on a bed of tomato braised cauliflower.

Nutrition:
Calories: 290
Fat: 10 g
Carbohydrate: 13 g
Protein: 38 g

27

CHEESEBURGER SOUP

Preparation Time: 20 minutes
Cooking Time: 25 minutes
Servings: 4
Ingredients:
¼ cup of chopped onion
1 quantity of 14.5 oz. can diced tomato
1 lb. of 90% lean ground beef
¾ cup of diced celery
2 teaspoon of Worcestershire sauce
3 cups of low sodium chicken broth
¼ teaspoon of salt
1 teaspoon of dried parsley
7 cups of baby spinach
¼ teaspoon of ground pepper
4 oz. of reduced-fat shredded cheddar cheese
Directions:
Get a large soup pot and cook the beef until it becomes brown. Add the celery, onion, and sauté until it becomes tender. Remove from the fire and drain excess liquid.

Stir in the broth, tomatoes, parsley, Worcestershire sauce,

pepper, and salt. Cover and allow it to simmer on low heat for about 20 minutes

Add spinach and leave it to cook until it becomes wilted in about 1-3 minutes. Top each of your servings with 1 ounce of cheese.

Nutrition:
Calories: 400
Carbohydrate: 11 g
Protein: 44 g
Fat: 20 g

BRAISED COLLARD GREENS IN PEANUT SAUCE WITH PORK TENDERLOIN

Preparation Time: 20 minutes
Cooking Time: 1 hour 12 minutes
Servings: 4
Ingredients:
2 cups of chicken stock
12 cups of chopped collard greens
5 tablespoon of powdered peanut butter
3 cloves of garlic, crushed
1 teaspoon of salt
½ teaspoon of allspice
½ teaspoon of black pepper
2 teaspoon of lemon juice
¾ teaspoon of hot sauce
1 ½ lb. of pork tenderloin
Directions:
Get a pot with a tight-fitting lid and combine the collards with the garlic, chicken stock, hot sauce, and half of the pepper and salt. Cook on low heat for about 1 hour or until the collards become tender.

Once the collards are tender, stir in the allspice, lemon juice. And powdered peanut butter. Keep warm.

Season the pork tenderloin with the remaining pepper and salt, and broil in a toaster oven for 10 minutes when you have an internal temperature of 1450F. Make sure to turn the tenderloin every 2 minutes to achieve an even browning all over. After that, you can take away the pork from the oven and allow it to rest for like 5 minutes.

Slice the pork as you will

Nutrition:
Calories: 320
Fat: 10 g
Carbohydrate: 15 g
Protein: 45 g

LEAN AND GREEN RECIPES (DINNER) VEGETARIAN

29

TASTE OF NORMANDY SALAD

Preparation Time: 25 minutes
Cooking Time: 5 minutes
Servings: 4 to 6
Ingredients:
For the walnuts
2 tablespoons butter
¼ cup sugar or honey
1 cup walnut pieces
½ teaspoon kosher salt
For the dressing
3 tablespoons extra-virgin olive oil
1½ tablespoons champagne vinegar
1½ tablespoons Dijon mustard
¼ teaspoon kosher salt
For the salad
1 head red leaf lettuce, shredded into pieces
3 heads endive, ends trimmed and leaves separated
2 apples, cored and divided into thin wedges
1 (8-ounce) Camembert wheel, cut into thin wedges
Direction:

To make the walnuts

Dissolve the butter in a skillet over medium high heat. Stir in the sugar and cook until it dissolves. Add the walnuts and cook for about 5 minutes, stirring, until toasty. Season with salt and transfer to a plate to cool.

To make the dressing

Whip the oil, vinegar, mustard, and salt in a large bowl until combined.

To make the salad

Add the lettuce and endive to the bowl with the dressing and toss to coat. Transfer to a serving platter.

Decoratively arrange the apple and Camembert wedges over the lettuce and scatter the walnuts on top. Serve immediately.

Meal Prep Tip: Prepare the walnuts in advance—in fact, double the quantities and use them throughout the week to add a healthy crunch to salads, oats, or simply to enjoy as a snack.

Nutrition:

Calories: 699
Total fat: 52g
Total carbs: 44g
Cholesterol: 60mg
Fiber: 17g
Protein: 23g
Sodium: 1170mg

30

LOADED CAESAR SALAD WITH CRUNCHY CHICKPEAS

Preparation Time: 5 minutes
Cooking Time: 20 minutes
Servings: 6
Ingredient:
For the chickpeas
2 (15-ounce) cans chickpeas, drained and rinsed
2 tablespoons extra-virgin olive oil
1 teaspoon kosher salt
1 teaspoon garlic powder
1 teaspoon onion powder
1 teaspoon dried oregano
For the dressing
½ cup mayonnaise
2 tablespoons grated Parmesan cheese
2 tablespoons freshly squeezed lemon juice
1 clove garlic, peeled and smashed
1 teaspoon Dijon mustard
½ tablespoon Worcestershire sauce
½ tablespoon anchovy paste
For the salad

3 heads romaine lettuce, cut into bite-size pieces

Direction :

To make the chickpeas

Preheat the oven to 450°F. Line a baking sheet with parchment paper.

Add the chickpeas, oil, salt, garlic powder, onion powder, and oregano in a small container. Scatter the coated chickpeas on the prepared baking sheet.

Roast for about 20 minutes, tossing occasionally, until the chickpeas are golden and have a bit of crunch.

To make the dressing

In a small bowl, whisk the mayonnaise, Parmesan, lemon juice, garlic, mustard, Worcestershire sauce, and anchovy paste until combined.

To make the salad

Combine the lettuce and dressing in a large container. Toss to coat. Top with the roasted chickpeas and serve.

Cooking Tip: Don't wash out that bowl you used for the chickpeas—the remaining oil adds a great punch of flavor to blanched green beans or another simply cooked vegetable.

Nutrition:

Calories: 367

Total fat: 22g

Total carbs: 35g

Cholesterol: 9mg

Fiber: 13g

Protein: 12g

Sodium: 407mg

31

COLESLAW WORTH A SECOND HELPING

Preparation Time: 20 minutes
Cooking Time: 10 minutes
Servings: 6
Ingredients:
5 cups shredded cabbage
2 carrots, shredded
⅓ cup chopped fresh flat-leaf parsley
½ cup mayonnaise
½ cup sour cream
3 tablespoons apple cider vinegar
1 teaspoon kosher salt
½ teaspoon celery seed
Direction :
Add together the cabbage, carrots, and parsley in a large bowl.

Whisk together the mayonnaise, sour cream, vinegar, salt, and celery in a small bowl until smooth. Pour sauce over veggies and pour until covered. Transfer to a serving bowl and bake until ready to serve.

Nutrition:

Calories: 192
Total fat: 18g
Total carbs: 7g
Cholesterol: 18mg
Fiber: 3g
Protein: 2g
Sodium: 543mg

32

ROMAINE LETTUCE AND RADICCHIOS MIX

Preparation Time: 6 minutes
Cooking Time: 0 minutes
Servings: 4
Ingredients:
2 tablespoons olive oil
A pinch of salt and black pepper
2 spring onions, chopped
3 tablespoons Dijon mustard
Juice of 1 lime
½ cup basil, chopped
4 cups romaine lettuce heads, chopped
3 radicchios, sliced
Directions:
In a salad bowl, blend the lettuce with the spring onions and the other ingredients, toss and serve.
Nutrition:
Calories: 87
Fats: 2 g
Fiber: 1 g

Carbs: 1 g
Protein: 2 g

33

GREEK SALAD

Preparation Time: 15 Minutes
Cooking Time: 15 Minutes
Servings: 5
Ingredients:
For Dressing:
½ teaspoon black pepper
¼ teaspoon salt
½ teaspoon oregano
1 tablespoon garlic powder
2 tablespoons Balsamic
1/3 cup olive oil
For Salad:
½ cup sliced black olives
½ cup chopped parsley, fresh
1 small red onion, thin-sliced
1 cup cherry tomatoes, sliced
1 bell pepper, yellow, chunked
1 cucumber, peeled, quarter and slice
4 cups chopped romaine lettuce
½ teaspoon salt

2 tablespoons olive oil

Directions:

In a small container, join all of the ingredients for the dressing and let this set in the freezer while you make the salad.

To assemble the salad, mix together all the ingredients in a large-sized bowl and toss the veggies gently but thoroughly to mix.

Serve the salad with the dressing in amounts as desired

Nutrition:

Calories: 234
Fat: 16.1 g
Protein: 5 g
Carbs: 48 g

34

ASPARAGUS AND SMOKED SALMON SALAD

Preparation Time: 15 minutes
Cooking Time: 10 minutes
Servings: 8
Ingredients:
1 lb. fresh asparagus, shaped and cut into 1 inch pieces
1/2 cup pecans, smashed into pieces
2 heads red leaf lettuce, washed and split
1/2 cup frozen green peas, thawed
1/4 lb. smoked salmon, cut into 1 inch chunks
1/4 cup olive oil
2 tablespoons. lemon juice
1 teaspoon Dijon mustard
1/2 teaspoon salt
1/4 teaspoon pepper
Directions:
Boil a pot of water. Stir in asparagus and cook for 5 minutes until tender. Let it drain; set aside.

In a skillet, cook the pecans over medium heat for 5 minutes, stirring constantly until lightly toasted.

Combine the asparagus, toasted pecans, salmon, peas, and red leaf lettuce and toss in a large bowl.

In another bowl, combine lemon juice, pepper, Dijon mustard, salt, and olive oil. You can coat the salad with the dressing or serve it on its side.

Nutrition:
Calories: 159
Total Carbohydrate: 7 g
Cholesterol: 3 mg
Total Fat: 12.9 g
Protein: 6 g
Sodium: 304 mg

35

SHRIMP COBB SALAD

Preparation Time: 25 minutes
Cooking Time: 10 minutes
Servings: 2
Ingredients:
4 slices center-cut bacon
1 lb. large shrimp, peeled and deveined
1/2 teaspoon ground paprika
1/4 teaspoon ground black pepper
1/4 teaspoon salt, divided
2 1/2 tablespoons. Fresh lemon juice
1 1/2 tablespoons. Extra-virgin olive oil
1/2 teaspoon whole grain Dijon mustard
1 (10 oz.) package romaine lettuce hearts, chopped
2 cups cherry tomatoes, quartered
1 ripe avocado, cut into wedges
1 cup shredded carrots
Directions:
Cook the bacon for 4 minutes on each side in a large skillet over medium heat till crispy.

Take away from the skillet and place on paper towels; let cool for 5 minutes. Break the bacon into bits. Throw out most of the bacon fat, leaving behind only 1 tablespoon. in the skillet. Bring the skillet back to medium-high heat. Add black pepper and paprika to the shrimp for seasoning. Cook the shrimp around 2 minutes each side until it is opaque. Sprinkle with 1/8 teaspoon of salt for seasoning.

Combine the remaining 1/8 teaspoon of salt, mustard, olive oil and lemon juice together in a small bowl. Stir in the romaine hearts.

On each serving plate, place on 1 and 1/2 cups of romaine lettuce. Add on top the same amounts of avocado, carrots, tomatoes, shrimp and bacon.

Nutrition:
Calories: 528
Total Carbohydrate: 22.7 g
Cholesterol: 365 mg
Total Fat: 28.7 g
Protein: 48.9 g
Sodium: 1166 mg

36

TOAST WITH SMOKED SALMON, HERBED CREAM CHEESE, AND GREENS

Preparation Time: 10 minutes
Cooking Time: 5 minutes
Servings: 2
Ingredients:
For the herbed cream cheese
¼ cup cream cheese, at room temperature
2 tablespoons chopped fresh flat-leaf parsley
2 tablespoons chopped fresh chives or sliced scallion
½ teaspoon garlic powder
¼ teaspoon kosher salt
For the toast
2 slices bread
4 ounces smoked salmon
Small handful microgreens or sprouts
1 tablespoon capers, drained and rinsed
¼ small red onion, very thinly sliced
Directions:
To make the herbed cream cheese
In a small container, put together the cream cheese, parsley,

chives, garlic powder, and salt. Using a fork, mix until combined. Chill until ready to use.

To make the toast

Toast the bread until golden. Spread the herbed cream cheese over each piece of toast, then top with the smoked salmon.

Garnish with the microgreens, capers, and red onion.

Nutrition:

Calories: 194

Total fat: 8g

Cholesterol: 26mg

Fiber: 2g

Protein: 12g

Sodium: 227mg

37
CRAB MELT WITH AVOCADO AND EGG

Preparation Time: 15 minutes
Cooking Time: 15 minutes
Servings: 2
Ingredients:
2 English muffins, split
3 tablespoons butter, divided
2 tomatoes, cut into slices
1 (4-ounce) can lump crabmeat
6 ounces sliced or shredded cheddar cheese
4 large eggs
Kosher salt
2 large avocados, halved, pitted, and cut into slices
Microgreens, for garnish
Directions:
Preheat the broiler.

Toast the English muffin halves. Place the toasted halves, cut-side up, on a baking sheet.

Spread 1½ teaspoons of butter evenly over each half, allowing the butter to melt into the crevices. Top each with tomato slices, then divide the crab over each, and finish with the cheese.

Boil for about 4 minutes until the cheese melts.

Meanwhile, in a medium skillet over medium heat, melt the remaining 1 tablespoon of butter, swirling to coat the bottom of the skillet. Crack the eggs into the skillet, giving ample space for each. Sprinkle with salt. Cook for about 3 minutes. Turn the eggs and cook the other side until the yolks are set to your liking. Place a egg on each English muffin half.

Top with avocado slices and microgreens.

Nutrition:
Calories: 1221
Total fat: 84g
Cholesterol: 94mg
Fiber: 2g
Protein: 12g
Sodium: 888mg

38

CRISPY POTATOES WITH SMOKED SALMON, KALE, AND HOLLANDAISE-STYLE SAUCE

Preparation Time: 15 minutes
Cooking Time: 15 minutes
Servings: 2
Ingredients:
2 tablespoons extra-virgin olive oil, plus additional for preparing the baking sheet
½ recipe roasted potatoes
8ounces mushrooms, stemmed and sliced
1 garlic clove, minced
8ounces kale, thick stems removed, leaves cut into 2-inch pieces
Kosher salt
Freshly ground black pepper
½ recipe Hollandaise-Style Sauce, at room temperature
8 ounces smoked salmon
Directions:
Preheat the oven to 400°F. Lightly coat a baking sheet with oil.
Place the roasted potatoes on the prepared baking sheet and heat until warm.
Heat the oil over medium heat until it shimmers. Add the

mushrooms and sauté for about 4 minutes until softened. Add the garlic and cook for 30 seconds. Add the kale and sauté for about 5 minutes until wilted and soft. Season with salt and pepper.

In a large bowl, combine the warmed potatoes and the kale and mushroom mixture. Toss to combine. Divide between 2 plates and spoon the sauce on top.

Nestle the salmon next to the vegetables on each plate and serve.

Nutrition:
Calories: 705
Total fat: 42g
Cholesterol: 47mg
Fiber: 12g
Protein: 15g
Sodium: 427mg

LEAN AND GREEN RECIPES (DESSERT)

39

FARO WITH ARTICHOKE HEARTS

Preparation Time: 10 minutes
Cooking Time: 40 minutes
Servings: 6
Ingredients:
1 cup faro
1 bay leaf
1 fresh rosemary sprig
1 fresh thyme sprig
2 tablespoons extra-virgin olive oil
1 onion, chopped
2 cups frozen artichoke hearts, thawed and chopped
1 tablespoon Italian seasoning
3 garlic cloves, minced
2 cups unsalted vegetable broth
Zest of 1 lemon
½ teaspoon sea salt
⅛ teaspoon freshly ground black pepper
¼ cup (about 2 ounces) grated Parmesan cheese
Directions:
In a medium pot, combine the faro, bay leaf, rosemary, and

thyme with enough water to cover it by about 2 inches. Place it on the stove top over medium-high heat and bring it to a boil. Reduce the heat to medium-low and simmer uncovered for 25 to 30 minutes, stirring occasionally, until the grain is tender. Drain any excess water and set the faro aside. Remove and discard the bay leaf, rosemary, and thyme.

In a large skillet over medium-high heat, heat the olive oil until it shimmers.

Add the onion, artichoke hearts, and Italian seasoning. Cook for about 5 minutes, stirring frequently, until the onion is soft.

Add the garlic and cook for 30 seconds, stirring constantly.

Add the broth, ½ cup at a time, and stir constantly until the liquid is absorbed before adding the next ½ cup of broth.

Stir in the lemon zest, sea salt, pepper, and cheese. Cook for 1 to 2 minutes more, stirring, until the cheese melts.

Nutrition:

Calories: 138
Protein: 7g
Total Carbohydrates: 11g
Sugars: 2g
Fiber: 2g
Total Fat: 8g
Saturated Fat: 2g
Cholesterol: 8mg
Sodium: 522mg

40

RICE AND SPINACH

Preparation Time: 10 minutes
Cooking Time: 15 minutes
Servings: 6
Ingredients:
2 tablespoons extra-virgin olive oil
1 onion, chopped
4 cups fresh baby spinach
1 garlic clove, minced
Zest of 1 orange
Juice of 1 orange
1 cup unsalted vegetable broth
½ teaspoon sea salt
⅛ teaspoon freshly ground black pepper
2 cups cooked brown rice
Directions:
In a large skillet over medium-high heat, heat the olive oil until it shimmers.

Add the onion and cook for about 5 minutes, stirring occasionally, until soft.

Add the spinach and cook for about 2 minutes, stirring occasionally, until it wilts.

Add the garlic and cook for 30 seconds, stirring constantly.

Stir in the orange zest and juice, broth, sea salt, and pepper. Bring to a simmer.

Stir in the rice and cook for about 4 minutes, stirring, until the rice is heated through and the liquid is absorbed.

Nutrition:

Calories: 188

Protein: 4g

Total Carbohydrates: 31g

Sugars: 4g

Fiber: 3g

Total Fat: 6g

Saturated Fat: 1g

Cholesterol: 0mg

Sodium: 301mg

41

SPICED COUSCOUS

Preparation Time: 10 minutes
Cooking Time: 15 minutes
Servings: 6
Ingredients:
2 tablespoons extra-virgin olive oil
½ onion, minced
Juice of 1 orange
Zest of 1 orange
½ teaspoon garlic powder
½ teaspoon ground cumin
½ teaspoon sea salt
¼ teaspoon ground ginger
¼ teaspoon ground allspice
¼ teaspoon ground cinnamon
⅛ teaspoon freshly ground black pepper
2 cups water
1 cup whole-wheat couscous
¼ cup dried apricots, chopped
¼ cup dried cranberries
Directions:

In a medium saucepan over medium-high heat, heat the olive oil until it shimmers.

Add the onion and cook for about 3 minutes, stirring occasionally, until soft.

Add the orange juice and zest, garlic powder, cumin, sea salt, ginger, allspice, cinnamon, pepper, and water. Bring to a boil.

Add the couscous, apricots, and cranberries. Stir once, turn off the heat, and cover the pot. Let rest for 5 minutes, covered. Fluff with a fork.

Nutrition:
Calories: 181
Protein: 6g
Total Carbohydrates: 30g
Sugars: 5g
Fiber: 4g
Total Fat: 6g
Saturated Fat: 1g
Cholesterol: 0mg
Sodium: 157mg

SWEET POTATO MASH

Preparation Time: 10 minutes
Cooking Time: 20 minutes
Servings: 6
Ingredients:
4 sweet potatoes, peeled and cubed
¼ cup almond milk
¼ cup extra-virgin olive oil
½ teaspoon sea salt
⅛ teaspoon freshly ground black pepper
Directions:

In a large pot over high heat, combine the sweet potatoes with enough water to cover by 2 inches. Bring the water to a boil. Reduce the heat to medium and cover the pot. Cook for 15 to 20 minutes until the potatoes are soft.

Drain the potatoes and return them to the dry pot off the heat. Add the almond milk, olive oil, sea salt, and pepper. With a potato masher, mash until smooth.

Nutrition:
Calories: 243
Protein: 2g

Total Carbohydrates: 35g
Sugars: 5g
Fiber: 5g
Total Fat: 11g
Saturated Fat: 3g
Cholesterol: 0mg
Sodium: 169mg

43

TABBOULEH

Preparation Time: 10 minutes
Cooking Time: 0 minutes
Servings: 6
Ingredients:
2 cups cooked whole-wheat couscous, cooled completely (see tip)
12 cherry tomatoes, quartered
6 scallions, white and green parts, minced
1 cucumber, peeled and chopped
½ cup fresh Italian parsley leaves, chopped
½ cup fresh mint leaves, chopped
Juice of 2 lemons
¼ cup extra-virgin olive oil
½ teaspoon sea salt
¼ teaspoon freshly ground black pepper
Directions:
In a large bowl, combine the couscous, tomatoes, scallions, cucumber, parsley, and mint. Set aside.
In a small bowl, whisk the lemon juice, olive oil, sea salt, and

pepper. Toss with the couscous mixture. Let sit for 1 hour before serving.

Nutrition:
Calories: 254
Protein: 8g
Total Carbohydrates: 38g
Sugars: 9g
Fiber: 7g
Total Fat: 10g
Saturated Fat: 2g
Cholesterol: 0mg
Sodium: 181mg

44

ORZO WITH SPINACH AND FETA

Preparation Time: 25 minutes
Cooking Time: 0 minutes
Servings: 6
Ingredients:
6 cups fresh baby spinach, chopped
¼ cup scallions, white and green parts, chopped
1 (16-ounce) package orzo pasta, cooked according to package directions, rinsed, drained, and cooled
¾ cup crumbled feta cheese
¼ cup halved Kalamata olives
½ cup red wine vinegar
¼ cup extra-virgin olive oil
1½ teaspoons freshly squeezed lemon juice
Sea salt
Freshly ground black pepper
Directions:
In a large bowl, combine the spinach, scallions, and cooled orzo.
Sprinkle with the feta and olives.

In a small bowl, whisk the vinegar, olive oil, and lemon juice. Season with sea salt and pepper.

Add the dressing to the salad and gently toss to combine. Refrigerate until serving.

Nutrition:
Calories: 255
Protein: 8g
Total Carbohydrates: 38g
Sugars: 3g
Fiber: 2g
Total Fat: 8g
Saturated Fat: 2g
Cholesterol: 5mg
Sodium: 279mg

45

PASTA PUTTANESCA

Preparation Time: 10 minutes
Cooking Time: 10 minutes
Ingredients:
2 tablespoons extra-virgin olive oil
6 garlic cloves, finely minced (or put through a garlic press)
2 teaspoons anchovy paste
¼ teaspoon red pepper flakes, plus more as needed
20 black olives, pitted and chopped
3 tablespoons capers, drained and rinsed
¼ teaspoon sea salt
¼ teaspoon freshly ground black pepper
2 (14-ounce) cans crushed tomatoes, undrained
1 (14-ounce) can chopped tomatoes, drained
¼ cup chopped fresh basil leaves
8 ounces' whole-wheat spaghetti, cooked according to package rinsed and drained

Directions:
In a sauté pan or skillet over medium heat, stir together the olive oil, garlic, anchovy paste, and red pepper flakes. Cook for about 2 minutes, stirring, until the mixture is very fragrant.

Add the olives, capers, sea salt, and pepper.

In a blender, purée the crushed and chopped tomatoes and add to the pan. Cook for about 5 minutes, stirring occasionally, until the mixture simmers.

Stir in the basil and cooked pasta. Toss to coat the pasta with the sauce and serve.

Nutrition:
Calories: 278
Protein: 10g
Total Carbohydrates: 40g
Sugars: 16g
Fiber: 12g
Total Fat: 13g
Saturated Fat: 1g
Cholesterol: 9mg
Sodium: 1,099mg

46

PASTA WITH PESTO

Preparation Time: 10 minutes
Cooking Time: 0 minutes
Servings: 4
Ingredients:
3 tablespoons extra-virgin olive oil
3 garlic cloves, finely minced
½ cup fresh basil leaves
¼ cup (about 2 ounces) grated Parmesan cheese
¼ cup pine nuts
8 ounces' whole-wheat pasta, cooked according to package drained

Directions:
In a blender or food processor, combine the olive oil, garlic, basil, cheese, and pine nuts. Pulse for 10 to 20 (1-second) pulses until everything is chopped and blended.

Toss with the hot pasta and serve.

Nutrition:
Calories: 405
Protein: 13g
Total Carbohydrates: 44g

Sugars: 2g
Fiber: 5g
Total Fat: 21g
Saturated Fat: 4g
Cholesterol: 10mg
Sodium: 141mg

47

SUN-DRIED TOMATO AND ARTICHOKE PIZZA

Preparation Time: 30 minutes
Cooking Time: 25 minutes
Servings: 6
Ingredients:
¾ cup whole-wheat flour, plus more for flouring the work surface
¾ cup all-purpose flour
1 package quick-rising yeast
¾ teaspoon sea salt
⅔ cup hot water (120°F to 125°F)
2 tablespoons extra-virgin olive oil
¼ teaspoon honey
Nonstick cooking spray

For The Sauce:
2 tablespoons extra-virgin olive oil
½ onion, minced
3 garlic cloves, minced
1 (14-ounce) can crushed tomatoes
1 tablespoon dried oregano

For The Pizza:
1 cup oil-packed sun-dried tomatoes, rinsed
2 cups frozen artichoke hearts
¼ cup (about 2 ounces) grated Asiago cheese

Directions:

In a medium bowl, whisk the whole-wheat and all-purpose flours, yeast, and salt.

In a small bowl, whisk the hot water, olive oil, and honey.

Mix the liquids into the flour mixture and stir until sticky ball forms.

Turn the dough out onto a floured surface and knead for 5 minutes.

Coat a sheet of plastic wrap with cooking spray and cover the dough. Let rest for 10 minutes.

Roll the dough into a 13-inch circle.

In a saucepan over medium-high heat, heat the olive oil until it shimmers.

Add the onion and cook for 5 minutes, stirring occasionally.

Add the garlic and cook for 30 seconds, stirring constantly.

Stir in the tomatoes and oregano. Bring to a simmer. Reduce the heat to medium-low and simmer for 5 minutes more.

Preheat the oven to 500°F (or the hottest setting).

If you have a pizza stone, place it in the oven as it preheats.

In a thin layer, spread the sauce over the rolled dough.

Top the sauce with the artichoke hearts and sun-dried tomatoes. Sprinkle the cheese lightly over the top.

Place the pizza on the stone (or directly on the rack) and bake for 10 to 15 minutes until the crust is golden.

Nutrition:
Calories: 318
Protein: 12g
Total Carbohydrates: 39g
Sugars: 5g
Fiber: 6g
Total Fat: 14g

Saturated Fat: 3g
Cholesterol: 7mg
Sodium: 524mg

LEAN AND GREEN RECIPES (SNACKS)

48

VEGGIE FRITTERS

Preparation Time: 10 minutes
Cooking Time: 10 minutes
Servings: 4
Ingredients:
2 garlic cloves, minced
2 yellow onions, chopped
4 scallions, chopped
2 carrots, grated
2 teaspoons cumin, ground
½ teaspoon turmeric powder
Salt and black pepper to the taste
¼ teaspoon coriander, ground
2 tablespoons parsley, chopped
¼ teaspoon lemon juice
½ cup almond flour
2 beets, peeled and grated
2 eggs, whisked
¼ cup tapioca flour
3 tablespoons olive oil
Directions:

In a bowl, combine the garlic with the onions, scallions and the rest of the ingredients except the oil, stir well and shape medium fritters out of this mix.

Heat oil in a pan over medium-high heat, add the fritters, cook for 5 minutes on each side, arrange on a platter and serve.

Nutrition:
Calories 209
Fat 11.2 g
Fiber 3 g
Carbs 4.4 g
Protein 4.8 g

49

WHITE BEAN DIP

Preparation Time: 10 minutes
Cooking Time: 0 minute
Servings: 4
Ingredients:
15 ounces canned white beans, drained and rinsed
6 ounces canned artichoke hearts, drained and quartered
4 garlic cloves, minced
1 tablespoon basil, chopped
2 tablespoons olive oil
Juice of ½ lemon
Zest of ½ lemon, grated
Salt and black pepper to the taste

Directions:
In your food processor, combine the beans with the artichokes and the rest of the ingredients except the oil and pulse well.

Add the oil gradually, pulse the mix again, divide into cups and serve as a party dip.

Nutrition:
Calories 274

Fat 11.7 g
Fiber 6.5 g
Carbs 18.5 g
Protein 16.5 g

50

EGGPLANT DIP

Preparation Time: 10 minutes
Cooking Time: 40 minutes
Servings: 4
Ingredients:
1 eggplant, poked with a fork
2 tablespoons tahini paste
2 tablespoons lemon juice
2 garlic cloves, minced
1 tablespoon olive oil
Salt and black pepper to the taste
1 tablespoon parsley, chopped
Directions:
Put the eggplant in a roasting pan, bake at 400° F for 40 minutes, cool down, peel and transfer to your food processor.

Add the rest of the remaining ingredients except the parsley, pulse well, divide into small bowls and serve as an appetizer with the parsley sprinkled on top.

Nutrition:
Calories 121

Fat 4.3 g
Fiber 1 g
Carbs 1.4 g
Protein 4.3 g

51

BULGUR LAMB MEATBALLS

Preparation Time: 10 minutes
Cooking Time: 15 minute
Servings: 6
Ingredients:
1 and ½ cups Greek yogurt
½ teaspoon cumin, ground
1 cup cucumber, shredded
½ teaspoon garlic, minced
A pinch of salt and black pepper
1 cup bulgur
2 cups water
1 pound lamb, ground
¼ cup parsley, chopped
¼ cup shallots, chopped
½ teaspoon allspice, ground
½ teaspoon cinnamon powder
1 tablespoon olive oil

Directions:
Combine the bulgur with the water in a bowl, cover the bowl, leave aside for 10 minutes, drain and transfer to a bowl.

Add the meat, the yogurt and the rest of the ingredients except the oil, stir well and shape medium meatballs out of this mix.

Heat oil in a pan over medium-high heat, add the meatballs, cook them for 7 minutes on each side, arrange them all on a platter and serve as an appetizer.

Nutrition:
Calories 300
Fat 9.6 g
Fiber 4.6 g
Carbs 22.6 g
Protein 6.6 g

52

CUCUMBER BITES

Preparation Time: 10 minutes
Cooking Time: 0 minutes
Servings: 12
Ingredients:
1 English cucumber, sliced into 32 rounds
10 ounces hummus
16 cherry tomatoes, halved
1 tablespoon parsley, chopped
1 ounce feta cheese, crumbled
Directions:
Spread the hummus on each cucumber round, divide the tomato halves on each, sprinkle the cheese and parsley on to and serve as an appetizer.
Nutrition:
Calories 162
Fat 3.4 g
Fiber 2 g
Carbs 6.4 g
Protein 2.4 g

53

STUFFED AVOCADO

Preparation Time: 10 minutes
Cooking Time: 0 minute
Servings: 2
Ingredients:
1 avocado, halved and pitted
10 ounces canned tuna, drained
2 tablespoons sun-dried tomatoes, chopped
1 and ½ tablespoon basil pesto
2 tablespoons black olives, pitted and chopped
Salt and black pepper to the taste
2 teaspoons pine nuts, toasted and chopped
1 tablespoon basil, chopped

Directions:
Combine the tuna with the sun-dried tomatoes in a bowl, and the rest of the ingredients except the avocado and stir.

Stuff the avocado halves with the tuna mix and serve as an appetizer.

Nutrition:
Calories 233

Fat 9 g
Fiber 3.5 g
Carbs 11.4 g
Protein 5.6 g

54

HUMMUS WITH GROUND LAMB

Preparation Time: 10 minutes
Cooking Time: 15 minute
Servings: 8
Ingredients:
10 ounces hummus
12 ounces lamb meat, ground
½ cup pomegranate seeds
¼ cup parsley, chopped
1 tablespoon olive oil
Pita chips for serving

Directions:
Heat oil in a pan over medium-high heat, add the meat, and brown for 15 minutes stirring often.

Spread the hummus on a platter, spread the ground lamb all over, also spread the pomegranate seeds and the parsley and serve with pita chips as a snack.

Nutrition:
Calories 133
Fat 9.7 g

Fiber 1.7 g
Carbs 6.4 g
Protein 5 g

55

WRAPPED PLUMS

Preparation Time: 5 minutes
Cooking Time: 0 minutes
Servings: 8
Ingredients:
2 ounces prosciutto, cut into 16 pieces
4 plums, quartered
1 tablespoon chives, chopped
A pinch of red pepper flakes, crushed
Directions:
Wrap each plum quarter in a prosciutto slice, arrange them all on a platter, sprinkle the chives and pepper flakes all over and serve.
Nutrition:
Calories 30
Fat 1 g
Fiber 0 g
Carbs 4 g
Protein 2 g

CUCUMBER SANDWICH BITES

Preparation Time: 5 minutes
Cooking Time: 0 minutes
Servings: 12
Ingredients:
1 cucumber, sliced
8 slices whole wheat bread
2 tablespoons cream cheese, soft
1 tablespoon chives, chopped
¼ cup avocado, peeled, pitted and mashed
1 teaspoon mustard
Salt and black pepper to the taste
Directions:
Spread the mashed avocado on each bread slice, also spread the rest of the ingredients except the cucumber slices. Divide the cucumber slices on the bread slices, cut each slice in thirds, arrange on a platter and serve as an appetizer.
Nutrition:
Calories 187
Fat 12.4 g

Fiber 2.1 g
Carbs 4.5 g
Protein 8.2 g

57

CUCUMBER ROLLS

Preparation Time: 5 minutes
Cooking Time: 0 minutes
Servings: 6
Ingredients:
1 big cucumber, sliced lengthwise
1 tablespoon parsley, chopped
8 ounces canned tuna, drained and mashed
Salt and black pepper to the taste
1 teaspoon lime juice
Directions:
Arrange cucumber slices on a working surface, divide the rest of the ingredients, and roll.
Arrange all the rolls on a surface and serve as an appetizer.
Nutrition:
Calories 200
Fat 6 g
Fiber 3.4 g
Carbs 7.6 g
Protein 3.5 g

58

OLIVES AND CHEESE STUFFED TOMATOES

Preparation Time: 10 minutes
Cooking Time: 0 minutes
Servings: 24
Ingredients:
24 cherry tomatoes, top cut off and insides scooped out
2 tablespoons olive oil
¼ teaspoon red pepper flakes
½ cup feta cheese, crumbled
2 tablespoons black olive paste
¼ cup mint, torn
Directions:
In a bowl, mix the olives paste with the rest of the ingredients except the cherry tomatoes and whisk well. Stuff the cherry tomatoes with this mix, arrange them all on a platter and serve as an appetizer.
Nutrition:
Calories 136
Fat 8.6 g
Fiber 4.8 g

Carbs 5.6 g
Protein 5.1 g

59

TOMATO SALSA

Preparation Time: 5 minutes
Cooking Time: 0 minutes
Servings: 6
Ingredients:
1 garlic clove, minced
4 tablespoons olive oil
5 tomatoes, cubed
1 tablespoon balsamic vinegar
¼ cup basil, chopped
1 tablespoon parsley, chopped
1 tablespoon chives, chopped
Salt and black pepper to the taste
Pita chips for serving
Directions:
Mix the tomatoes with the garlic in a bowl, and the rest of the ingredients except the pita chips, stir, divide into small cups and serve with the pita chips on the side.
Nutrition:
Calories 160

Fat 13.7 g
Fiber 5.5 g
Carbs 10.1 g
Protein 2.2

60
CHILI MANGO AND WATERMELON SALSA

Preparation Time: 5 minutes
Cooking Time: 0 minutes
Servings: 12
Ingredients:
1 red tomato, chopped
Salt and black pepper to the taste
1 cup watermelon, seedless, peeled and cubed
1 red onion, chopped
2 mangos, peeled and chopped
2 chili peppers, chopped
¼ cup cilantro, chopped
3 tablespoons lime juice
Pita chips for serving

Directions:
In a bowl, mix the tomato with the watermelon, the onion and the rest of the ingredients except the pita chips and toss well. Divide the mix into small cups and serve with pita chips on the side.

Nutrition:

Calories 62
Fat g
Fiber 1.3 g
Carbs 3.9 g
Protein 2.3 g

61

CREAMY SPINACH AND SHALLOTS DIP

Preparation Time: 10 minutes
Cooking Time: 0 minutes
Servings: 4
Ingredients:
1 pound spinach, roughly chopped
2 shallots, chopped
2 tablespoons mint, chopped
¾ cup cream cheese, soft
Salt and black pepper to the taste

Directions:
Combine the spinach with the shallots and the rest of the ingredients in a blender,, and pulse well. Divide into small bowls and serve as a party dip.

Nutrition:
Calories 204
Fat 11.5 g
Fiber 3.1 g
Carbs 4.2 g
Protein 5.9 g

62

FETA ARTICHOKE DIP

Preparation Time: 10 minutes
Cooking Time: 30 minutes
Servings: 8
Ingredients:
8 ounces artichoke hearts, drained and quartered
¾ cup basil, chopped
¾ cup green olives, pitted and chopped
1 cup parmesan cheese, grated
5 ounces feta cheese, crumbled
Directions:
In your food processor, mix the artichokes with the basil and the rest of the ingredients, pulse well, and transfer to a baking dish.

Introduce in the oven, bake at 375° F for 30 minutes and serve as a party dip.

Nutrition:
Calories 186
Fat 12.4 g
Fiber 0.9 g

Carbs 2.6 g
Protein 1.5 g

63

AVOCADO DIP

Preparation Time: 5 minutes
Cooking Time: 0 minutes
Servings: 8
Ingredients:
½ cup heavy cream
1 green chili pepper, chopped
Salt and pepper to the taste
4 avocados, pitted, peeled and chopped
1 cup cilantro, chopped
¼ cup lime juice
Directions:
Pour the cream with the avocados and the rest of the ingredients in a blender, and pulse well. Divide the mix into bowls and serve cold as a party dip.
Nutrition:
Calories 200
Fat 14.5 g
Fiber 3.8 g
Carbs 8.1 g
Protein 7.6 g

64

GOAT CHEESE AND CHIVES SPREAD

Preparation Time: 10 minutes
Cooking Time: 0 minute
Servings: 4
Ingredients:
2 ounces goat cheese, crumbled
¾ cup sour cream
2 tablespoons chives, chopped
1 tablespoon lemon juice
Salt and black pepper to the taste
2 tablespoons extra virgin olive oil
Directions:
Mix the goat cheese with the cream and the rest of the ingredients in a bowl, and whisk really well. Keep in the fridge for 10 minutes and serve as a party spread.
Nutrition:
Calories 220
Fat 11.5 g
Fiber 4.8 g
Carbs 8.9 gProtein 5.6 g

FUELING RECIPES (BREAKFAST)

65

LETTUCE SALAD WITH BEEF STRIPS

Preparation Time: 10 minutes
Cooking Time: 12 minutes
Servings: 5
Ingredients:
2 cup lettuce
10 oz. beef brisket
2 tablespoon sesame oil
1 tablespoon sunflower seeds
1 cucumber
1 teaspoon ground black pepper
1 teaspoon paprika
1 teaspoon Italian spices
2 teaspoon butter
1 teaspoon dried dill
2 tablespoon coconut milk
Directions:
Cut the beef brisket into strips.
Sprinkle the beef strips with the ground black pepper, paprika, and dried dill.
Preheat the air fryer to 365 F.

Put the butter in the air fryer basket tray and melt it.

Then add the beef strips and cook them for 6 minutes on each side.

Meanwhile, tear the lettuce and toss it in a big salad bowl.

Crush the sunflower seeds and sprinkle over the lettuce.

Chop the cucumber into the small cubes and add to the salad bowl.

Then combine the sesame oil and Italian spices together. Stir the oil.

Combine the lettuce mixture with the coconut milk and stir it using 2 wooden spatulas.

When the meat is cooked – let it chill to room temperature.

Add the beef strips to the salad bowl.

Stir it gently and sprinkle the salad with the sesame oil dressing.

Serve the dish immediately.

Nutrition:
Calories: 199
Fat: 12.4g
Carbs: 3.9g
Protein: 18.1g

CAYENNE RIB EYE STEAK

Preparation Time: 10 minutes
Cooking Time: 13 minutes
Servings: 2
Ingredients:
1-pound rib eye steak
1 teaspoon salt
1 teaspoon cayenne pepper
½ teaspoon chili flakes
3 tablespoon cream
1 teaspoon olive oil
1 teaspoon lemongrass
1 tablespoon butter
1 teaspoon garlic powder
Directions:
Preheat the air fryer to 360 F.

Take a shallow bowl and combine the cayenne pepper, salt, chili flakes, lemongrass, and garlic powder together.

Mix the spices gently.

Sprinkle the rib eye steak with the spice mixture.

Melt the butter and combine it with cream and olive oil.

Churn the mixture.

Pour the churned mixture into the air fryer basket tray.

Add the rib eye steak.

Cook the steak for 13 minutes. Do not stir the steak during the cooking.

When the steak is cooked transfer it to a paper towel to soak all the excess fat.

Serve the steak. You can slice the steak if desired.

Nutrition:

Calories: 708

Fat: 59g

Carbs: 2.3g

Protein: 40.4g

67

BEEF-CHICKEN MEATBALL CASSEROLE

Preparation Time: 15 minutes
Cooking Time: 21 minutes
Servings: 7
Ingredients:
1 eggplant
10 oz. ground chicken
8 oz. ground beef
1 teaspoon minced garlic
1 teaspoon ground white pepper
1 tomato
1 egg
1 tablespoon coconut flour
8 oz. Parmesan, shredded
2 tablespoon butter
1/3 cup cream
Directions:
Combine the ground chicken and ground beef in a large bowl.

Add the minced garlic and ground white pepper.

In the bowl Crack the egg with the ground meat mixture and stir it carefully until well combined.

Then add the coconut flour and mix.

Make small meatballs from the ground meat.

Preheat the air fryer to 360 F.

Sprinkle the air fryer basket tray with the butter and pour the cream.

Peel the eggplant and chop it.

Put the meatballs over the cream and sprinkle them with the chopped eggplant.

Slice the tomato and place it over the eggplant.

Make a layer of shredded cheese over the sliced tomato.

Put the casserole in the air fryer and cook it for 21 minutes.

Let the casserole cool to room temperature before serving.

Nutrition:

Calories: 314

Fat: 16.8g

Carbs: 7.5g

Protein: 33.9g

68

JUICY PORK CHOPS

Preparation Time: 10 minutes
Cooking Time: 11 minutes
Servings: 3
Ingredients:
1 teaspoon peppercorns
1 teaspoon kosher salt
1 teaspoon minced garlic
½ teaspoon dried rosemary
1 tablespoon butter
13 oz. pork chops
Directions:
Rub the pork chops with the dried rosemary, minced garlic, and kosher salt.

Preheat the air fryer to 365 F.

Put the butter and peppercorns in the air fryer basket tray. Melt the butter.

Place the pork chops in the melted butter.

Cook the pork chops for 6 minutes.

Turn the pork chops over.

Cook the pork chops for 5 minutes more.

When the meat is cooked dry gently with the paper towel. Serve the juicy pork chops immediately.
Nutrition:
Calories: 431,
Fat: 34.4g
Carbs: 0.9g
Protein: 27.8

69

CHICKEN GOULASH

Preparation Time: 10 minutes
Cooking Time: 17 minutes
Servings: 6
Ingredients:
4 oz. chive stems
2 green peppers, chopped
1 teaspoon olive oil
14 oz. ground chicken
2 tomatoes
½ cup chicken stock
2 garlic cloves, sliced
1 teaspoon salt
1 teaspoon ground black pepper
1 teaspoon mustard
Directions:
Chop chives roughly.
Spray the air fryer basket tray with the olive oil.
Preheat the air fryer to 365 F.
Put the chopped chives in the air fryer basket tray.

Add the chopped green pepper and cook the vegetables for 5 minutes.

Add the ground chicken.

Chop the tomatoes into the small cubes and add them in the air fryer mixture too.

Cook the mixture for 6 minutes more.

Add the chicken stock, sliced garlic cloves, salt, ground black pepper, and mustard.

Mix well to combine.

Cook the goulash for 6 minutes more.

Nutrition:
Calories: 161
Fat: 6.1g
Carbs: 6g
Protein: 20.3g

CHICKEN & TURKEY MEATLOAF

Preparation Time: 15 minutes
Cooking Time: 25 minutes
Servings: 12
Ingredients:
3 tablespoon butter
10 oz. ground turkey
7 oz. ground chicken
1 teaspoon dried dill
½ teaspoon ground coriander
2 tablespoons almond flour
1 tablespoon minced garlic
3 oz. fresh spinach
1 teaspoon salt
1 egg
½ tablespoon paprika
1 teaspoon sesame oil
Directions:
Put the ground turkey and ground chicken in a large bowl.

Sprinkle the meat with dried dill, ground coriander, almond flour, minced garlic, salt, and paprika.

Then chop the fresh spinach and add it to the ground poultry mixture.

break the egg into the meat mixture and mix well until you get a smooth texture.

Great the air fryer basket tray with the olive oil.

Preheat the air fryer to 350 F.

Roll the ground meat mixture gently to make the flat layer.

Put the butter in the center of the meat layer.

Make the shape of the meatloaf from the ground meat mixture. Use your fingertips for this step.

Place the meatloaf in the air fryer basket tray.

Cook for 25 minutes.

When the meatloaf is cooked allow it to rest before serving.

Nutrition:
Calories: 142
Fat: 9.8 g
Carbs: 1.7g
Protein: 13g

71

TURKEY MEATBALLS WITH DRIED DILL

Preparation Time: 15 minutes
Cooking Time: 11 minutes
Servings: 9
Ingredients:
1-pound ground turkey
1 teaspoon chili flakes
¼ cup chicken stock
2 tablespoon dried dill
1 egg
1 teaspoon salt
1 teaspoon paprika
1 tablespoon coconut flour
2 tablespoons heavy cream
1 teaspoon olive oil
Directions:
In a bowl, whisk the egg with a fork.
Add the ground turkey and chili flakes.
Sprinkle the mixture with dried dill, salt, paprika, coconut flour, and mix it up.
Make the meatballs from the ground turkey mixture.

Preheat the air fryer to 360 F.

Grease the air fryer basket tray with the olive oil.

Then put the meatballs inside.

Cook the meatballs for 6 minutes – for 3 minutes on each side.

Sprinkle the meatballs with the heavy cream.

Cook the meatballs for 5 minutes more.

When the turkey meatballs are cooked – let them rest for 2-3 minutes.

Nutrition:

Calories: 124

Fat: 7.9g

Carbs: 1.2g

Protein: 14.8g

72

CHICKEN COCONUT POPPERS

Preparation Time: 10 minutes
Cooking Time: 10 minutes
Servings: 6
Ingredients:
½ cup coconut flour
1 teaspoon chili flakes
1 teaspoon ground black pepper
1 teaspoon garlic powder
11 oz. chicken breast, boneless, skinless
1 tablespoon olive oil
Directions:
Cut the chicken breast into sizeable cubes and put them in a large bowl.

Sprinkle the chicken cubes with the chili flakes, ground black pepper, garlic powder, and stir them well using your hands.

After this, sprinkle the chicken cubes with the almond flour.

Shake the bowl with the chicken cubes gently to coat the meat.

Preheat the air fryer to 365 F.

Grease the air fryer basket tray with the olive oil.

Place the chicken cubes inside.
Cook the chicken poppers for 10 minutes.
Turn the chicken poppers over after 5 minutes of cooking.
Allow the cooked chicken poppers to cool before serving.

Nutrition:
Calories: 123
Fat: 4.6g
Carbs: 6.9g
Protein: 13.2g

73

PARMESAN BEEF SLICES

Preparation Time: 14 minutes
Cooking Time: 25 minutes
Servings: 4
Ingredients:
12 oz. beef brisket
1 teaspoon kosher salt
7 oz. Parmesan, sliced
5 oz. chive stems
1 teaspoon turmeric
1 teaspoon dried oregano
2 teaspoon butter
Directions:
Slice the beef brisket into 4 slices.
Sprinkle every beef slice with the turmeric and dried oregano.
Grease the air fryer basket tray with the butter.
Put the beef slices inside.
Dice the chives.
Make a layer using the diced chives over the beef slices.
Then make a layer using the Parmesan cheese.
Preheat the air fryer to 365 F.

Cook the beef slices for 25 minutes.
Nutrition:
Calories: 348
Fat: 18g
Carbs: 5g
Protein: 42.1g

74

CHILI BEEF JERKY

Preparation Time: 25 minutes
Cooking Time: 2.5 hours
Servings: 6
Ingredients:
14 oz. beef flank steak
1 teaspoon chili pepper
3 tablespoon apple cider vinegar
1 teaspoon ground black pepper
1 teaspoon onion powder
1 teaspoon garlic powder
¼ teaspoon liquid smoke
Directions:
Slice the beefsteak into the medium strips and then tenderize each piece.

Take a bowl and combine the apple cider vinegar, ground black pepper, onion powder, garlic powder, and liquid smoke.

Whisk gently with a fork.

Then transfer the beef pieces in the mixture and stir well.

Leave the meat to marinade for up to 8 hours.

Put the marinated beef pieces in the air fryer rack.

Cook the beef jerky for 2.5 hours at 150 F.
Nutrition:
Calories: 129
Fat: 4.1g
Carbs: 1.1g
Protein: 20.2 g

75

SPINACH BEEF HEART

Preparation Time: 15 minutes
Cooking Time: 20 minutes
Servings: 4
Ingredients:
1-pound beef heart
5 oz. chive stems
½ cup fresh spinach
1 teaspoon salt
1 teaspoon ground black pepper
3 cups chicken stock
1 teaspoon butter
Directions:
Remove all the fat from the beef heart.
Dice the chives.
Chop the fresh spinach.
Combine the diced chives, fresh spinach, and butter together. Stir it.
Make a cut in the beef heart and fill it with the spinach-chives mixture.
Preheat the air fryer to 400 F.

Pour the chicken stock into the air fryer basket tray.

Sprinkle the Prepared stuffed beef heart with the salt and ground black pepper.

Put the beef heart in the air fryer and cook it for 20 minutes.

Remove the cooked heart from the air fryer and slice it.

Sprinkle the slices with the remaining liquid from the air fryer.

Nutrition:

Calories: 216

Fat: 6.8g

Fiber: 0.8g

Carbs: 3.8gProtein: 33.3

FUELING RECIPES (MAIN MEAL)

76

PARMESAN ZUCCHINI ROUNDS

Preparation Time: 25 minutes
Cooking Time: 20 minutes
Servings: 4
Ingredients:
4 zucchinis; sliced
1 ½ cups parmesan; grated
¼ cup parsley; chopped.
1 egg; whisked
1 egg white; whisked
½ tsp. garlic powder
Cooking spray
Directions:
Take a bowl and mix the egg with egg whites, parmesan, parsley and garlic powder and whisk.

Dredge each zucchini slice in this mix, place them all in your air fryer's basket, grease them with cooking spray and cook at 370°F for 20 minutes

Divide between plates and serve as a side dish.
Nutrition:

Calories: 183
Fat: 6g
Fiber: 2g
Carbs: 3g
Protein: 8g

77

GREEN BEAN CASSEROLE

Preparation Time: 25 minutes
Cooking Time: 20 minutes
Servings: 4
Ingredients:
1 lb. fresh green beans, edges trimmed
½ oz. pork rinds, finely ground
1 oz. full-fat cream cheese
½ cup heavy whipping cream.
¼ cup diced yellow onion
½ cup chopped white mushrooms
½ cup chicken broth
4 tbsp. unsalted butter.
¼ tsp. xanthan gum
Directions:
Over heat melt the butter in a skillet.

Sauté the onion and mushrooms until soft and fragrant, about 3-5 minutes.

Add the heavy cream, cream cheese, and broth to the skillet. Lightly beat until smooth. Boil and then simmer. Put the xanthan gum in the pan and remove from heat

Cut green beans into 2-inch pieces and place in 4-cup round pan. Pour sauce mixture over them and stir until covered. Fill the plate with ground pork rinds. Place in the fryer basket

Set the temperature to 320 degrees F and set the timer for 15 minutes. The top will be a golden and green bean fork when fully cooked. Serve hot.

Nutrition:
Calories: 267
Protein: 3.6g
Fat: 23.4g
Carbs: 9.7g

ZUCCHINI SPAGHETTI

Preparation Time: 20 minutes
Cooking Time: 15 minutes
Servings: 4
Ingredients:
1 lb. zucchinis, cut with a spiralizer
1 cup parmesan; grated
¼ cup parsley; chopped.
¼ cup olive oil
6 garlic cloves; minced
½ tsp. red pepper flakes
Salt and black pepper to taste.
Directions:
In a pan that fits your air fryer, mix all the ingredients, toss, introduce in the fryer and cook at 370°F for 15 minutes
Divide between plates and serve as a side dish.
Nutrition:
Calories: 200
Fat: 6g
Carbs: 4g
Protein: 5g

79

CABBAGE AND RADISHES MIX

Preparation Time: 20 minutes
Cooking Time: 15 minutes
Servings: 4
Ingredients:
6 cups green cabbage; shredded
½ cup celery leaves; chopped.
¼ cup green onions; chopped.
6 radishes; sliced
3 tbsp. olive oil
2 tbsp. balsamic vinegar
½ tsp. hot paprika
1 tsp. lemon juice
Directions:
In your air fryer's pan, combine all the ingredients and toss well.

Place the pan in the fryer and cook at 380°F for 15 minutes. Divide between plates and serve as a side dish

Nutrition:
Calories: 130

Fat: 4g
Carbs: 4g
Protein: 7g

80

KALE CHIPS

Preparation Time: 10 minutes
Cooking Time: 5 minutes
Servings: 4
Ingredients:
4 cups stemmed kale
½ tsp. salt
2 tsp. avocado oil
Directions:
Take a large bowl, sprinkle the cabbage in avocado oil, and sprinkle with salt. Place in the fryer basket.

Set the temperature to 400 degrees F and set the timer for 5 minutes. The kale will be crispy when done. Serve immediately.

Nutrition:
Calories: 25
Protein: 0.5g
Fat: 2.2g
Carbs: 1.1g

81

CORIANDER ARTICHOKES

Preparation Time: 20 minutes
Cooking Time: 15 minutes
Servings: 4
Ingredients:
12 oz. artichoke hearts
1 tbsp. lemon juice
1 tsp. coriander, ground
½ tsp. cumin seeds
½ tsp. olive oil
Salt and black pepper to taste.
Directions:
In a pan that fits your air fryer, mix all the ingredients, toss, introduce the pan in the fryer and cook at 370°F for 15 minutes
Divide the mix between plates and serve as a side dish.
Nutrition:
Calories: 200
Fat: 7g
Carbs: 5g
Protein: 8g

82

SPINACH AND ARTICHOKES SAUTÉ

Preparation Time: 20 minutes
Cooking Time: 15 minutes
Servings: 4
Ingredients:
10 oz. artichoke hearts; halved
2 cups baby spinach
3 garlic cloves
¼ cup veggie stock
2 tsp. lime juice
Salt and black pepper to taste.
Directions:
In a pan that fits your air fryer, mix all the ingredients, toss, introduce in the fryer and cook at 370°F for 15 minutes
Divide between plates and serve as a side dish.
Nutrition:
Calories: 209
Fat: 6g
Carbs: 4g
Protein: 8g

83

GREEN BEANS

Preparation Time: 5 minutes
  Cooking Time: 20 minutes Servings: 4
Ingredients:
6 cups green beans; trimmed
1 tbsp. hot paprika
2 tbsp. olive oil
A pinch of salt and black pepper
Directions:
Take a bowl and mix the green beans with the other ingredients, toss, put them in the air fryer's basket and cook at 370°F for 20 minutes

Divide between plates and serve as a side dish.
Nutrition:
Calories: 120
Fat: 5g
Carbs: 4g
Protein: 2g

84

BALSAMIC CABBAGE

Preparation Time: 10 minutes
Cooking Time: 15 minutes
Servings: 4
Ingredients:
6 cups red cabbage; shredded
4 garlic cloves; minced
1 tbsp. olive oil
1 tbsp. balsamic vinegar
Salt and black pepper to taste.
Directions:
In a pan that fits the air fryer, combine all the ingredients, toss, introduce the pan in the oven and cook at 380°F for 15 minutes
Divide between plates and serve as a side dish.
Nutrition:
Calories: 151
Fat: 2g
Carbs: 5g
Protein: 5g

85

HERBED RADISH SAUTÉ

Preparation Time: 5 minutes
Cooking Time: 15 minutes
Servings: 4
Ingredients:
2 bunches red radishes; halved
2 tbsp. parsley; chopped.
2 tbsp. balsamic vinegar
1 tbsp. olive oil
Salt and black pepper to taste.
Directions:
Take a bowl and mix the radishes with the remaining ingredients except the parsley, toss and put them in your air fryer's basket.

Cook at 400°F for 15 minutes, divide between plates, sprinkle the parsley on top and serve as a side dish

Nutrition:
Calories: 180
Fat: 4g
Carbs: 3g
Protein: 5g

86

ROASTED TOMATOES

Preparation Time: 5 minutes
Cooking Time: 15 minutes
Servings: 4
Ingredients:
4 tomatoes; halved
½ cup parmesan; grated
1 tbsp. basil; chopped.
½ tsp. onion powder
½ tsp. oregano; dried
½ tsp. smoked paprika
½ tsp. garlic powder
Cooking spray

Directions:
Mix all the ingredients in a bowl and except the cooking spray and the parmesan.

Arrange the tomatoes in your air fryer's pan, sprinkle the parmesan on top and grease with cooking spray

Cook at 370°F for 15 minutes, divide between plates and serve.

Nutrition:
Calories: 200
Fat: 7g
Carbs: 4g
Protein: 6g

KALE AND WALNUTS

Preparation Time: 5 minutes
Cooking Time: 15 minutes
Servings: 4
Ingredients:
3 garlic cloves
10 cups kale; roughly chopped.
1/3 cup parmesan; grated
½ cup almond milk
¼ cup walnuts; chopped.
1 tbsp. butter; melted
¼ tsp. nutmeg, ground
Salt and black pepper to taste.
Directions:
In a pan that fits the air fryer, combine all the ingredients, toss, introduce the pan in the machine and cook at 360°F for 15 minutes

Divide between plates and serve.
Nutrition:
Calories: 160

Fueling Recipes (Main meal)

Fat: 7g
Carbs: 4g
Protein: 5g

88

BOK CHOY AND BUTTER SAUCE

Preparation Time: 5 minutes
Cooking Time: 15 minutes
Servings: 4
Ingredients:
2 bok choy heads; trimmed and cut into strips
1 tbsp. butter; melted
2 tbsp. chicken stock
1 tsp. lemon juice
1 tbsp. olive oil
A pinch of salt and black pepper
Directions:
In a pan that fits your air fryer, mix all the ingredients, toss, introduce the pan in the oven and cook at 380°F for 15 minutes.
Divide between plates and serve as a side dish
Nutrition:
Calories: 141
Fat: 3g
Carbs: 4g
Protein: 3g

89

TURMERIC MUSHROOM

Preparation Time: 5 minutes
Cooking Time: 15 minutes
Servings: 4
Ingredients:
1 lb. brown mushrooms
4 garlic cloves; minced
¼ tsp. cinnamon powder
1 tsp. olive oil
½ tsp. turmeric powder
Salt and black pepper to taste.
Directions:
In a bowl, combine all the ingredients and toss.
Put the mushrooms in your air fryer's basket and cook at 370°F for 15 minutes
Divide the mix between plates and serve as a side dish.
Nutrition:
Calories: 208
Fat: 7g
Carbs: 5g
Protein: 7g

FUELING RECIPES (SNACKS AND DESSERT)

90

CHOCOLATE BARS

Preparation Time: 10 minutes
Cooking Time: 20 minutes
Servings: 16
Ingredients:
15 oz cream cheese, softened
15 oz unsweetened dark chocolate
1 tsp vanilla
10 drops liquid stevia
Directions:
Grease 8-inch square dish and set aside.
In a saucepan dissolve chocolate over low heat.
Add stevia and vanilla and stir well.
Remove pan from heat and set aside.
Add cream cheese into the blender and blend until smooth.
Add melted chocolate mixture into the cream cheese and blend until just combined.
Transfer mixture into the prepared dish and spread evenly and place in the refrigerator until firm.
Slice and serve.
Nutrition:

Calories: 230
Fat: 24 g
Carbs: 7.5 g
Sugar: 0.1 g
Protein: 6 g
Cholesterol: 29 mg

91
BLUEBERRY MUFFINS

Preparation Time: 15 minutes
Cooking Time: 35 minutes
Servings: 12
Ingredients:
2 eggs
1/2 cup fresh blueberries
1 cup heavy cream
2 cups almond flour
1/4 tsp lemon zest
1/2 tsp lemon extract
1 tsp baking powder
5 drops stevia
1/4 cup butter, melted
Directions:
heat the cooker to 350 F. Line muffin tin with cupcake liners and set aside.

Add eggs into the bowl and whisk until mix.

Add remaining ingredients and mix to combine.

Pour mixture into the prepared muffin tin and bake for 25 minutes.

Serve and enjoy.
Nutrition:
Calories: 190
Fat: 17 g
Carbs: 5 g
Sugar: 1 g
Protein: 5 g
Cholesterol: 55 mg

92

CHIA PUDDING

Preparation Time: 20 minutes
Cooking Time: 0 minutes
Servings: 2
Ingredients:
4 tbsp chia seeds
1 cup unsweetened coconut milk
1/2 cup raspberries
Directions:
Add raspberry and coconut milk into a blender and blend until smooth.

Pour mixture into the glass jar.

Add chia seeds in a jar and stir well.

Seal the jar with a lid and shake well and place in the refrigerator for 3 hours.

Serve chilled and enjoy.
Nutrition:
Calories: 360
Fat: 33 g
Carbs: 13 g

Sugar: 5 g
Protein: 6 g
Cholesterol: 0 mg

AVOCADO PUDDING

Preparation Time: 20 minutes
Cooking Time: 0 minutes
Servings: 8
Ingredients:
2 ripe avocados, pitted and cut into pieces
1 tbsp fresh lime juice
14 oz can coconut milk
2 tsp liquid stevia
2 tsp vanilla
Directions:
Inside the blender Add all ingredients and blend until smooth. Serve immediately and enjoy.
Nutrition:
Calories: 317
Fat: 30 g
Carbs: 9 g
Sugar: 0.5 g
Protein: 3 g
Cholesterol: 0 mg

94

PEANUT BUTTER COCONUT POPSICLE

Preparation Time: 15 minutes
Cooking Time: 0 minutes
Servings: 12
Ingredients:
1/2 cup peanut butter
1 tsp liquid stevia
2 cans unsweetened coconut milk
Directions:
In the blender add all the listed ingredients and blend until smooth.

Pour mixture into the Popsicle molds and place in the freezer for 4 hours or until set.

Serve and enjoy.
Nutrition:
Calories: 155
Fat: 15 g
Carbs: 4 g
Sugar: 2 g
Protein: 3 g
Cholesterol: 0 mg

DELICIOUS BROWNIE BITES

Preparation Time: 20 minutes
Cooking Time: 0 minutes
Servings: 13
Ingredients:
1/4 cup unsweetened chocolate chips
1/4 cup unsweetened cocoa powder
1 cup pecans, chopped
1/2 cup almond butter
1/2 tsp vanilla
1/4 cup monk fruit sweetener
1/8 tsp pink salt
Directions:
Add pecans, sweetener, vanilla, almond butter, cocoa powder, and salt into the food processor and process until well combined.

Transfer brownie mixture into the large bowl. Add chocolate chips and fold well.

Make small round shape balls from brownie mixture and place onto a baking tray.

Place in the freezer for 20 minutes.

Serve and enjoy.

Nutrition:
Calories: 108
Fat: 9 g
Carbs: 4 g
Sugar: 1 g
Protein: 2 g
Cholesterol: 0 mg

96

PUMPKIN BALLS

Preparation Time: 15 minutes
Cooking Time: 0 minutes
Servings: 18
Ingredients:
1 cup almond butter
5 drops liquid stevia
2 tbsp coconut flour
2 tbsp pumpkin puree
1 tsp pumpkin pie spice
Directions:
Mix together pumpkin puree in a large bowl, and almond butter until well combined.

Add liquid stevia, pumpkin pie spice, and coconut flour and mix well.

Make small balls from mixture and place onto a baking tray.

Place in the freezer for 1 hour.

Serve and enjoy.
Nutrition:
Calories: 96

Fat: 8 g
Carbs: 4 g
Sugar: 1 g
Protein: 2 g
Cholesterol: 0 mg

97

SMOOTH PEANUT BUTTER CREAM

Preparation Time: 10 minutes
Cooking Time: 0 minutes
Servings: 8
Ingredients:
1/4 cup peanut butter
4 overripe bananas, chopped
1/3 cup cocoa powder
1/4 tsp vanilla extract
1/8 tsp salt
Directions:
In the blender add all the listed ingredients and blend until smooth.
Serve immediately and enjoy.
Nutrition:
Calories: 101
Fat: 5 g
Carbs: 14 g
Sugar: 7 g
Protein: 3 g
Cholesterol: 0 mg

98

VANILLA AVOCADO POPSICLES

Preparation Time: 20 minutes
Cooking Time: 0 minutes
Servings: 6
Ingredients:
2 avocadoes
1 tsp vanilla
1 cup almond milk
1 tsp liquid stevia
1/2 cup unsweetened cocoa powder
Directions:
In the blender add all the listed ingredients and blend smoothly.

Pour blended mixture into the Popsicle molds and place in the freezer until set.

Serve and enjoy.
Nutrition:
Calories: 130
Fat: 12 g
Carbs: 7 g

Sugar: 1 g
Protein: 3 g
Cholesterol: 0 mg

99

CHOCOLATE POPSICLE

Preparation Time: 20 minutes
Cooking Time: 10 minutes
Servings: 6
Ingredients:
4 oz unsweetened chocolate, chopped
6 drops liquid stevia
1 1/2 cups heavy cream
Directions:
Add heavy cream into the microwave-safe bowl and microwave until just begins the boiling.

Add chocolate into the heavy cream and set aside for 5 minutes.

Add liquid stevia into the heavy cream mixture and stir until chocolate is melted.

Pour mixture into the Popsicle molds and place in freezer for 4 hours or until set.

Serve and enjoy.
Nutrition:
Calories: 198

Fat: 21 g
Carbs: 6 g
Sugar: 0.2 g
Protein: 3 g
Cholesterol: 41 mg

100

RASPBERRY ICE CREAM

Preparation Time: 10 minutes
Cooking Time: 0 minutes
Servings: 2
Ingredients:
1 cup frozen raspberries
1/2 cup heavy cream
1/8 tsp stevia powder
Directions:
Blend all the listed ingredients in a blender until smooth. Serve immediately and enjoy.
Nutrition:
Calories: 144
Fat: 11 g
Carbs: 10 g
Sugar: 4 g
Protein: 2 g
Cholesterol: 41 mg

101

CHOCOLATE FROSTY

Preparation Time: 20 minutes
Cooking Time: 0 minutes
Servings: 4
Ingredients:
2 tbsp unsweetened cocoa powder
1 cup heavy whipping cream
1 tbsp almond butter
5 drops liquid stevia
1 tsp vanilla
Directions:
Add cream into the medium bowl and beat using the hand mixer for 5 minutes.

Add remaining ingredients and blend until thick cream form.

Pour in serving bowls and place them in the freezer for 30 minutes.

Serve and enjoy.
Nutrition:
Calories: 137
Fat: 13 g

Carbs: 3 g
Sugar: 0.5 g
Protein: 2 g
Cholesterol: 41 mg

102

CHOCOLATE ALMOND BUTTER BROWNIE

Preparation Time: 10 minutes
Cooking Time: 16 minutes
Servings: 4
Ingredients:
1 cup bananas, overripe
1/2 cup almond butter, melted
1 scoop protein powder
2 tbsp unsweetened cocoa powder
Directions:
Preheat the air fryer to 325 F. Grease air fryer baking pan and set aside.
Blend all ingredients in a blender until smooth.
Pour batter into the prepared pan and place in the air fryer basket and cook for 16 minutes.
Serve and enjoy.
Nutrition:
Calories: 82
Fat: 2 g
Carbs: 11 g

Sugar: 5 g
Protein: 7 g
Cholesterol: 16 mg

103

PEANUT BUTTER FUDGE

Preparation Time: 10 minutes
Cooking Time: 10 minutes
Servings: 20
Ingredients:
1/4 cup almonds, toasted and chopped
12 oz smooth peanut butter
15 drops liquid stevia
3 tbsp coconut oil
4 tbsp coconut cream
Pinch of salt
Directions:
Line baking tray with parchment paper.

Melt coconut oil in a pan over low heat. Add peanut butter, coconut cream, stevia, and salt in a saucepan. Stir well.

Pour fudge mixture into the prepared baking tray and sprinkle chopped almonds on top.

Place the tray in the refrigerator for 1 hour or until set.

Slice and serve.
Nutrition:
Calories: 131

Fat: 12 g
Carbs: 4 g
Sugar: 2 g
Protein: 5 g
Cholesterol: 0 mg

104

ALMOND BUTTER FUDGE

Preparation Time: 10 minutes
Cooking Time: 10 minutes
Servings: 18
Ingredients:
3/4 cup creamy almond butter
1 1/2 cups unsweetened chocolate chips
Directions:
Line 8*4-inch pan with parchment paper and set aside.

Add chocolate chips and almond butter into the double boiler and cook over medium heat until the chocolate-butter mixture is melted. Stir well.

Place mixture into the prepared pan and place in the freezer until set.

Slice and serve.
Nutrition:
Calories: 197
Fat: 16 g
Carbs: 7 g
Sugar: 1 g
Protein: 4 g Cholesterol: 0 mg

CONCLUSION

The Optavia Diet can be effectively used for rapid weight loss compared to other plans simply because of the offer made by —lean and green‖ meals and its few calories.

According to U.S. News and World Report, it listed Optavia on the number 2 position as the best diet for rapid weight loss. They tied with Keto, Atkins, and Weight Watchers.

However, the 2019 U.S. News and World Report Best Diets positioned the Optavia Diet on number 31 in the list of Best Diets overall and graded it as 2.7/5.

Optavia doesn't require much-exerted energy compared to its competitors such as Weight Watchers (here, you will have to master a system of points) or keto (here, you must assess and closely track macronutrients).

The coaching component of Optavia can be compared to Jenny Craig and Weight Watchers, both of which urge users to register for meet-ups to get the necessary support.

Due to the highly processed nature of the majority of foods available on the Optavia diet, it could pose a threat or challenge compared to the variety of whole, fresh foods you can consume on more self-sustainable plans such as Atkins.

Conclusion

The Optavia diet enables weight loss through one-on-one coaching, low carb homemade meals, and low-calorie prepackaged diets.

Although the initial 5&1 Plan is quite limiting, the 3&3 maintenance phase enables fewer processed snacks and a wider variety of food which tend to make it easier to lose weight and adhere to the program for sustenance in the long term.

Nevertheless, the diet is repetitive, costly, and doesn't cover all dietary needs. Another point is that extended calorie restriction may lead to nutrient deficiencies and other risky health concerns.

Although the program promotes fat loss and short-term weight loss, further research is required to evaluate the level of lifestyle changes it needs for long-term success.

The logic is that eating healthy recipes will make you feel full for a long time not similarly to foods that are high in carbohydrates and saturated fat. That's why it focuses on increasing the consumption of whole foods and reducing dependence on fast commercial foods and other unhealthy foods.

The program has earned worldwide acclaim for its ability to deliver sustainable results without complicating the meal program for people. It places very few restrictions on food and inspires people to choose a healthier version of their daily food without compromising on taste and nutrition.

Choosing the right diet or program had also become difficult as the industry flourished. Many diets claim to have specific health problems while helping a diet lose weight.

One of the diet programs that is constantly introduced to the market is the optavia diet program. It is one of the programs followed and is most effective in it.

Unlike other diets, the optavia diet is not designed for a specific health condition. It is designed according to the dietitian's needs, to achieve the ideal weight and the healthy lifestyle you want.

The optavia diet program is a stress-free and easy to follow program. It is a cool way to start a journey to your health.

CPSIA information can be obtained
at www.ICGtesting.com
Printed in the USA
LVHW082226210321
682037LV00002B/81